The tomb builders

IN WALES 4000-3000 BC

First published in 2006 by
National Museum Wales Books,
Cathays Park, Cardiff CF10 3NP, Wales.
www.museumwales.ac.uk
© The National Museum of Wales

Amgueddfa Cymru-National Museum Wales
is an Assembly Sponsored Public Body.

ISBN 0 7200 0568 X

Editing and production: Mari Gordon
Design: MO-Design.com
Printed by: Gomer Press
**Cover photography and photos on frontispiece,
this page, acknowledgements, introduction
and pages 140, 142, 145,149,150:** Ray Edgar

national
museum
wales

amgueddfa
cymru

Noddir gan
Lywodraeth
Cynulliad Cymru
Sponsored by
Welsh Assembly
Government

The tomb builders

IN WALES 4000-3000 BC

Steve Burrow
with illustrations by Jackie Chadwick and Tony Daly
and photography by Kevin Thomas and Jim Wild
(unless otherwise noted)

NATIONAL MUSEUM WALES BOOKS, 2006

acknowledgements

Generations of researchers have studied Wales's megalithic tombs and the artefacts found in them. I draw heavily on all their work throughout this book and have done my best to include their names whenever I describe their contributions. I am especially grateful to two researchers who have allowed me to paraphrase their discoveries in advance of publication: Dr Rick Schulting of Queen's University Belfast (radiocarbon dating of Bryn yr Hen Bobl and Gop Cave) and Professor Alasdair Whittle of Cardiff University (dating of Tinkinswood).

Many other colleagues have also offered advice and support, and I owe them all thanks (all National Museum of Wales, unless stated otherwise): Ruth Battye, Rebecca Brumbill, Bernice Cardi (Swansea Museum), Louise Carey, Evan Chapman, Professor Gabriel Cooney (University College Dublin), Dr Vicki Cummings (University of Central Lancashire), Mary Davis, Katrina Deering, Pip Diment, Dr Dyfed Elis-Gruffydd, Jennifer Evans, Russell Gray (University of Auckland), Adam Gwilt, Professor Denise Hodges (Northern Illinois University), Heather Jackson, Adrian James (Society of Antiquaries of London), John Kenyon, Rob Kruszynski (Natural History Museum), Dr Louise Loe (Bournemouth University), Frances Lynch (Bangor University), Beth McNeice (Royal College of Surgeons of England), Louise Mumford, Ken Murphy (Cambria Archaeology), Frank Prendergast (Dublin Institute of Technology), Tania Ruiz (Leicester University), Dr Jay Stock (Duckworth Laboratory, University of Cambridge) and Dr Mick Wysocki (University of Central Lancashire).

The bulk of the photography and illustrations are the work of Jackie Chadwick, Tony Daly, Kevin Thomas and Jim Wild, but the following individuals and organizations have also allowed their work to be used: Cadw, The Cambrian Archaeological Association, Simon Chaplin (Royal College of Surgeons of England), Professor Tim Darvill (Bournemouth University), Ralph Fyfe (Exeter University), Frances Lynch (Bangor University) and the Royal Commission on the Ancient and Historical Monuments of Wales.

Earlier versions of the text have benefited from comments and correction by: Edward Besly (National Museum of Wales), Ray Burrow, Shanon Burrow, Tim Darvill (Bournemouth University), Ian Fell (Media for Heritage), Ashley McAvoy (National Museum of Wales), Matthew Ritchie (Cadw) and Elizabeth Walker (National Museum of Wales).

It is a pleasure to also record my debt to Richard Brewer and Mark Redknap (both National Museum of Wales) who have encouraged and supported me throughout the research and writing of this book.

contents

introduction

Wales is a land filled with ancient monuments. Most obvious and best known are the castles that dominate so many high points and river crossings around the country. Some of these carry a history of Welsh pride and independence, others of English conquest and control. These are stories felt and understood by the tens of thousands of people who visit these sites every year. The many abbeys of Wales tell another story. Now largely roofless, their skeletal remains are potent symbols of religious life in the years before Henry VIII's dissolution of the monasteries in the mid-sixteenth century. Looking further back in time, Roman ruins and Iron Age hillforts tell tales of their own and, like other types of ancient monument, they attract thousands of visitors who want to share in these pieces of the past. But there is another type of monument, which keeps its place in history more closely guarded than the others: the megalithic tomb, also known as the dolmen or cromlech. These monumental structures of finely balanced stones and dark chambers are harder to decipher, yet they continue to attract a steady stream of visitors who come to feel their antiquity and enjoy their mystery. Megalithic tombs can be seen in all parts of Wales. Some, like Pentre Ifan in Pembrokeshire, are impressive for both their scale and drama. Others, like Bron y Foel Isaf in Gwynedd, are smaller and more intimate, a part of the landscape and not an attempt to dominate it. Many have been damaged, their stone skeletons exposed above a denuded cairn of stones, while others still remain sufficiently intact to allow the visitor the experience of walking down stone-lined passages into quiet chambers.

These tombs are found across Europe, from Spain to Scandinavia, but Wales, a land rich in building stone, is uniquely positioned to tell their story. Wales adjoins the lowlands of southern England and flanks the seaways that link Brittany to Ireland and western Scotland, so its inhabitants were exposed to the wide variety of ways of dealing with the dead found in other communities. Some of Wales's tombs bear witness to these

1

inter-regional links, others are more individual – innovations on a theme. It was not just styles of construction that the builders held in common with people in neighbouring areas, but the rituals of death as well: communities in south-east Wales shared a reverence for dry bones with people in southern England, while tomb builders in Anglesey decorated their tombs with a strange and unpredictable style of art found from northern Spain to Orkney.

This treasury of tombs has provided a fine resource for the many archaeologists who have studied these monuments over the course of the past century, and the National Museum of Wales has played a pivotal role in preserving their finds. Generations of researchers have visited the collections, and their work has enabled these silent stones to give up some of their secrets. Thanks to the efforts of these researchers, a great deal is known about the time of the construction of the tombs, the lives of their builders and the nature of the world in which they lived. This research has led to the rediscovery of a part of Wales's history that is both remote in time and foreign in substance.

dating the tombs

By the start of the nineteenth century, the time of the megalithic tombs had been completely forgotten: no historical records mentioned them, no folk memory preserved their story and their origins were wholly unknown.

An account written in 1723 by Henry Rowlands, an Anglican vicar, illustrates the problem. Henry Rowlands set out to write a history of Anglesey from earliest times. Working as he did in the days before Darwin and geological science, the tools he used were the Bible, linguistics (notably the similarities between words in different languages), the writings of Roman and more recent authors, folklore and his own observant eye. Taking the Bible at face value, he reasoned that the earliest surviving settlement must have been built after the biblical flood described in Genesis, since that event buried the land beneath waves and wiped the earth clean. The Bible also told him that the only people to have survived the flood were Noah and his family. Taking into account the approximate time it would have taken for Noah's descendants to repopulate the earth, Rowlands reasoned that it would have been Noah's grandchildren who first settled in Wales. The Bible also gave him reason to believe that the building of megalithic tombs was one of the first works they had undertaken on their arrival, because it says in Genesis 8: 20 that Noah's first act after the floodwaters had subsided was to 'build an altar unto the Lord' on which a sacrifice was laid.

In identifying megalithic tombs as sacrificial altars dating to the years after the biblical flood, Rowlands was simply writing history using the sources that seemed to him to be most reliable. It was only with the development of archaeology as a discipline that new sources of information were to become available to help determine the true origins of these sites. The first significant step forward came in 1836 when a Danish museum curator, Christian Jurgensen Thomsen, made an important discovery while sorting the pre-Roman collections at the National Museum of Denmark. Having examined a great quantity of artefacts from many different archaeological sites, he realized that objects made of stone were often found on sites without metal tools. This, he decided, must mean that there had once been a 'Stone Age', which preceded ages when metals were known. The recognition of a Stone Age followed by a Bronze Age and an Iron Age provided the beginnings of the chronology for prehistory we recognize today.

St Lythans megalithic tomb in the Vale of
Glamorgan. The term 'megalithic' is used
to describe a range of structures
constructed from large stones, of which
tombs, standing stones and stone circles
are among the best known. Megalithic
tombs are the earliest of these large stone
monuments in Wales.

From the eighteenth century these
monuments have been called 'cromlechs', a
Welsh word derived from 'crom' (crooked or
curved) and 'llech' (stone). Their French
name 'dolmen' has also been used in Wales
since the nineteenth century, although it is
less common today, except to describe a
particular style of tomb.

Throughout this book, the term 'megalithic
tomb' has been used, as it conveys both the
grandeur of these monuments (mega =
great, lith = stone) and their function as
houses for the dead.

The implications of Thomsen's discovery for the dating of Wales's megalithic tombs were realized by Edward Barnwell, Secretary of the Cambrian Archaeological Association. Writing in the Welsh journal *Archaeologia Cambrensis* in 1863, he noted that since bronze and iron tools were not found during excavations at megalithic tombs, these sites must belong to the Stone Age. The remote age of the tombs had been established: now all that remained was to determine when the Stone Age had been.

The answer to this question took another century to find. The breakthrough came as a result of work undertaken by Willard Libby at the University of Chicago. In 1949 he developed a method of dating organic materials based on the decay rate of the radioactive carbon atoms they contained. He tested his technique on objects of known age, such as wood from the coffins of Egyptian mummies and burnt bread from Pompeii. The results proved that his radiocarbon technique provided an accurate measure of age. Within a decade, laboratories that could utilize his new discovery had been established in Britain, and the process of dating British prehistory began.
By the early 1960s, the British Museum had dated charcoal from a tomb in Hampshire, and University College Dublin had dated a tomb in Ireland, while in 1964 Cambridge University published a date from a hearth associated with a megalith in Scotland.Cha Dates for Wales's tombs were slow in following, and the first did not appear until 1973, but the results so far obtained in Wales and from similar sites across the British Isles make it clear that the majority of megalithic tombs were constructed from shortly after 4000 BC and continued in use until at least 3000 BC. This means that the oldest tombs in Wales pre-date the Egyptian pyramids by 1,400 years; they are 2,000 years older than the first Chinese dynasties and 1,000 years older than the first Mesopotamian civilisations. Small wonder that Henry Rowlands found difficulty in dating these monuments using only the Bible and his own ingenuity.

the tomb builders

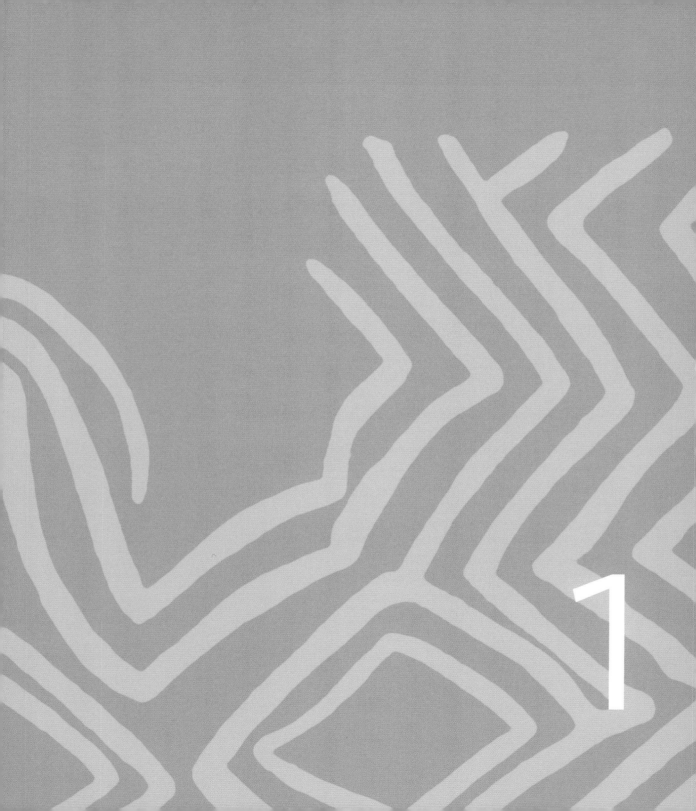

1

life before the megaliths

The research of the past two hundred years has focused not only on dating the tombs, but also on uncovering the reasons for their construction and the nature of the society that produced them. To do this, we must look still further back in time to an age before the construction of megaliths. Before 4000 BC, Wales was sparsely populated by small communities who lived in a land that was densely wooded from coast to coast. The lowlands were filled with oak, elm, lime and ash, their canopy probably only being broken by river courses and whatever man-made clearings could be maintained. This continuous canopy extended into the uplands, gradually thinning towards the mountain peaks. Seen from the air there would have been few signs of human occupation, just the occasional column of smoke rising from a fire and perhaps a few canoes moving along the coast.

Nonetheless, it was a rich landscape with much to offer those who lived in it. The woods were filled with wild animals, including herds of red deer, pigs and massive cattle known as aurochs. All were available as food if they could be caught. The woodland itself provided its share of food including hazelnuts, fruits, roots and seeds, while the rivers offered salmon, eels and other fish. Even honey was available for those brave enough to steal it from the bees. These resources offered a varied diet that was no doubt used to full advantage, yet not all these foods were available all year round. For example, hazelnuts were only available in autumn, although they could be preserved for longer, while salmon would have been most common over the summer and autumn months when they were migrating upriver to spawn. Even the herds of deer might have followed their own seasonal migrations between the uplands and lowlands.

All of these factors made it difficult for a community to stay in a single spot all year round. Instead, people probably moved from place to place, following an annual migration pattern that would take them to the right spot at the right time for the ripening of the next plant or to meet the moving deer herds. One way in which this

This illustration shows the distribution of sites in Wales known to have been in use between 9200 BC and 4000 BC. During this period, sea levels rose over 40m to reach their current height. It is likely, therefore, that many important occupation sites from this period have been lost to the waves.

© The National Museum of Wales (Tony Daly)

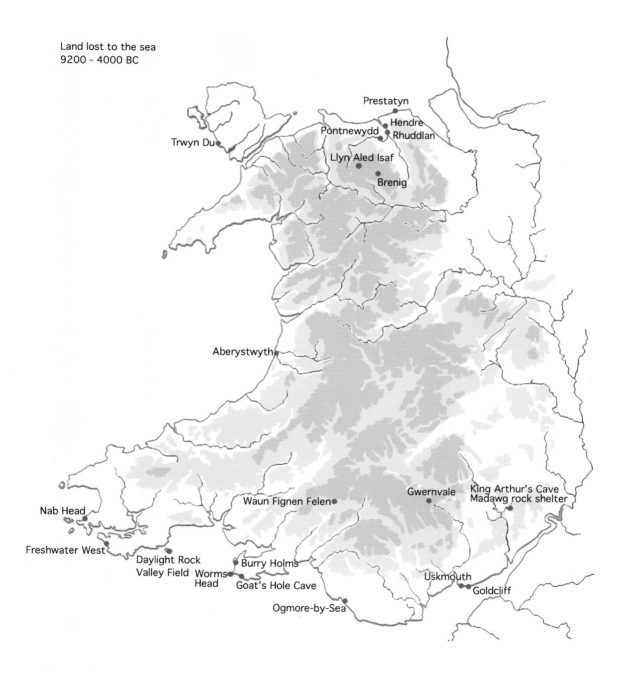

Land lost to the sea
9200 - 4000 BC

Prestatyn

Hendre

Pontnewydd

Rhuddlan

Trwyn Du

Llyn Aled Isaf

Brenig

Aberystwyth

Gwernvale

King Arthur's Cave

Madawg rock shelter

Nab Head

Waun Fignen Felen

Freshwater West

Daylight Rock

Valley Field

Burry Holms

Worms

Head

Goat's Hole Cave

Uskmouth

Goldcliff

Ogmore-by-Sea

Flint tools from Trwyn Du in Anglesey. Dating from around 7500 BC, this assortment of scrapers, adze-heads and barbs is typical of the range of equipment surviving from this period. The background illustrates the kinds of materials with which they were used.

© The National Museum of Wales (Jim Wild)

seasonal pattern might have been avoided was to live close to the coast, giving the community access to fish, shellfish and other constantly available foods. Unfortunately, sea levels have since risen, making it difficult to prove that such coastal settlements existed. What evidence there is for the consumption of seafood comes from the bones of the people who lived at this time. These have been found to contain chemical signatures that can only be obtained from fish and other marine foods.

The tools and other equipment made and used by these people to hunt, fish and gather plants would appear very basic by today's standards, but they were perfectly adapted to the tasks they served. The use of metals was unknown in Britain, leaving people reliant on raw materials such as wood, plant fibres, animal bones, antlers, sinews and stone. It was stone that formed the basis of their tool kits as some rocks, notably flint, could be flaked and shaped to produce sharp-edged implements that served as adze-heads, knives, scrapers and drills – implements necessary for the creation of more complex equipment. With these, wood could be worked to make handles for stone tools, bows and arrows and frames for shelters, backpacks and canoes. Stone tools could also be used to work more pliable plant fibres, turning them into baskets, ropes and netting. Another 'tool' available to people at this time was the dog. First domesticated from wolves during the Ice Age, the dog might have served as both a guard for the community and a hunting companion. Dog skeletons from the Stone Age period have been identified at sites in England, Scotland and Ireland, so it is likely that they were also present in Wales.

Using stone-tipped spears, bone harpoons, bows and arrows, and with the assistance of dogs, wild animals could be caught. As well as providing meat for food, their hides could then be cleaned and cured for clothing, bedding and the covering of shelters. Their sinews could also be used as twine to replace bow strings or for sewing, and their bones could be turned into tools. With equipment like this people found ways of surviving in a world that was still decidedly wild and untamed.

Dozens of occupation sites dating to this time have been excavated across Wales and the evidence discovered compares well with that from similar sites in the rest of

Britain and Ireland. At each one the evidence is slight, consisting for the most part of stone tools and ambiguous pits and hollows dug into the earth. Occasionally, the outline of a simple hut is found, revealed by a circle of holes where stakes had been driven into the earth, but these fragile finds are very rare in Britain and have yet to be discovered at all in Wales. It appears that people touched the earth only lightly, leaving little for us to find, and reinforcing the impression that life was lived on the move, travelling in search of food or living on the coast in settlements now lost.

Goldcliff, an area of coastal mudflats on the Severn Estuary near Newport, provides a good illustration of the kind of evidence that is available from such sites. Here, archaeologists recovered a range of flint tools and animal and fish bone as well as hazelnut shells and charcoal. Together, these finds suggest that during a winter around 5600 BC a small group visited the area, which was at that time a patch of raised ground surrounded by a reed swamp. They hunted red deer and pig, butchering their prey with stone tools. Burnt fish bones show that they also enjoyed meals of cooked eel. They did not stay at Goldcliff for very long, although where they went afterwards is unknown. Perhaps they carried their butchered kills back to a large family camp at another location, leaving behind a few bones to be discovered 7,000 years later. Or possibly this was their life – a series of short stays at productive hunting sites. Certainly, this was not the only time hunters and fishermen came to Goldcliff.

Many other sites in Wales tell similar stories. On the Black Mountain, at the western end of the Brecon Beacons, is a peat bog known as Waun Fignen Felen. This was once an upland lake, and at its edges small groups of hunters once lay in wait for thirsty animals coming to drink. They wiled away the idle moments by making new stone tools, leaving behind a scatter of flint and occasional stone beads. It is possible that upland hunting grounds like this and coastal camps like Goldcliff were used by the same communities, with the uplands providing prey when food was sparser elsewhere.

In Pembrokeshire, the headland known as The Nab Head has been excavated several times revealing evidence for a substantial settlement. One of the most important aspects of the archaeology at this site has been the discovery of stone beads, manufactured from flat pebbles found on the beaches beneath the headland. These were used to make bracelets or necklaces, and they serve as a reminder that life at this time did not consist solely of hunting, gathering and survival. Several hundred beads were found when this settlement was first excavated in 1925 and, if strung together as in the replica shown here right, these would have formed impressive jewellery.

Sites such as these are typical of many excavated by archaeologists studying this period. In combination, they build an image of a world where people lived according to the rhythms of the year. There is some evidence that people manipulated the landscape by burning areas of woodland, probably to encourage new plant growth that would in turn attract grazing animals; but for the most part they seem to have taken the world as they found it. Their lifestyle was stable and unchanging; sites in Wales dating from 9000 BC produce very similar evidence to those occupied 4,000 years later, around 5000 BC. It probably seemed to people at this time that life would continue in a similar way forever. However, in Continental Europe things were beginning to change.

Six 10,000-year-old beads from The Nab Head, a headland on the Pembrokeshire coast.

© The National Museum of Wales (Jim Wild)

megalithic tomb builders in Europe

By 8000 BC, in parts of western Asia such as the Zagros Mountains of Iran, Syria and around the Jordan valley, the seeds of a new life were already well-established as agricultural practices began to develop.

Signs of this process have been discovered at many sites across the Middle East. For example, at Jericho on the west bank of the Jordan valley there is evidence that people were not just relying on the seeds of wild grasses as a food source, but actually selecting the more productive plants so that they could enjoy better crops in the future. At Abu Hureyra in Syria, cultivated cereals were eaten and there is also evidence that people were no longer just hunting wild animals but had begun to herd sheep and goats. This process, carried on across the Middle East, led to the domestication of these and other species, and was the start of farming.

From our twenty-first-century perspective, the benefits of farming are clear. There is no need to move from place to place in search of the next meal, because it is always with you. When your fields of cereals and your herds of animals are large enough you can also sustain larger populations, not all of whom need be involved in the business of raising food. That relatively leisured group can then develop other skills – perhaps building, irrigation, trading or manufacture. The result is the civilisation we know today. This, at least, is the logic of farming, although the first people to select certain cereals and animals in preference to others could not have known that this would be the consequence of their actions.

Farming spread in every direction. In the Balkans, the migratory life of the hunter had given way to life in villages by 6000 BC. From about 5500 BC there were farming settlements across the central European plain based around clusters of long houses. By 4000 BC the British Isles and southern Scandinavia were the only parts of Western Europe where people continued to live their lives in the old ways; in all other parts of Continental Europe, farming was the dominant way of life. Across Europe many other aspects of human life began to change too. People were now able to settle in one area

The map shows the distribution of megalithic tombs in western Europe. The exact date at which this new burial ritual was adopted remains a subject of study in many parts of Europe. However, it can be said with certainty that tombs were in use in parts of Continental Europe for several hundred years before their first construction in Britain and Ireland shortly after 4000 BC.

© The National Museum of Wales (Tony Daly)

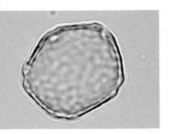

An elm tree pollen, about 0.035mm across. Pollen is remarkably pervasive and is often preserved in airless environments, such as in peat bogs or beneath deep spreads of soil. Since the pollen of each species of tree is different, it is possible to reconstruct past environments by studying the types of pollen preserved in suitable deposits.

Courtesy of Ralph Fyfe, Department of Geology pollen image database, University of Exeter

for longer, and in some regions this led to substantial houses being built in place of simple shelters. The types of tools people used also changed, with axes of polished stone becoming common and clay being used to make a new material: pottery. All this worked to change humanity's view of the world, leading to a growing expectation that nature could be domesticated and the wild places made to serve mankind's needs.

The building of tombs was a major part of this transformation. Whereas previously corpses were buried in graves or treated to other ephemeral burial rites, now they were given residences. By honouring their dead with permanent tombs, it seems that the living were stating their ownership of the land: 'our ancestors belong here, so this place is ours!'

This transformation seems to have begun around 4500 BC in two areas on the Atlantic coast of Europe: north-west Spain and Brittany. It is possible that tomb building in these areas grew from earlier rituals including burial within shell-middens, which might have served as markers in the landscape, or inhumation in rock-lined graves, which hints at the beginning of a link between the dead and stone.

In Britain at this time, farming, megalithic tombs, pottery and polished stone axes were still foreign concepts. It is likely that in the parts of Britain where people made good use of the resources of the sea, they would have received some news from abroad. However, there is no direct evidence of Continental goods being used in Britain before 4000 BC. Britain's position of isolation did not last, but the difficulty for archaeologists is in deciding when Britain rejoined the mainstream of European culture, how it did so and, most importantly, why.

In the centuries before 4000 BC, according to the environmental record, there was a marked decline in elm trees across Britain. This could be evidence that people were using the foliage of this tree as fodder for domestic animals, making this the first indirect evidence for herding in Britain. However, some scholars have argued that it is more likely to be evidence for an early form of Dutch elm disease – albeit one that seems to have struck different parts of the British Isles at different times. Pollen, possibly derived from domestic wheat and barley, has also been identified at sites across the British Isles dating as far back as 4900 BC, but once again there is uncertainty, as the pollen of wild grasses can be mistaken for those of domestic cereals.

The manufacture of pottery and the growing of cereals were innovations brought to Wales around 4000 BC.

© The National Museum of Wales (Jim Wild)

However, from about 4000 BC onwards all the hallmarks of the new Continental culture are to be found across the British Isles: farming, megalithic tombs, new flint tools and pottery. Using the chronologically coarse tools of the modern archaeologist, it appears as though the British Isles had been transformed overnight, although in reality the process was probably a very protracted one lasting generations. As to how it occurred, it has been suggested that farming communities on the Continent migrated into Britain, bringing their livestock and their new way of life across the English Channel and up the Irish Sea in hide-covered boats. If this were the case, the newly landed farmers might have quickly pushed back the indigenous people, establishing themselves and their way of life while the natives faded into oblivion. Alternatively, it has also been argued that the indigenous people might have decided that this new Continental lifestyle would be of benefit to them, and chosen to adopt it. Perhaps there was prestige to be had in feasting from new pottery bowls and in

offering neighbours a meal of bread, mutton, sheep or goat's milk, foods they might never have tasted before.

The truth is probably somewhere between these two extreme views and its discovery is likely to be brought nearer as techniques for the study of both ancient and modern DNA become more sophisticated. Archaeological evidence for farming in this period includes the bones of domestic sheep and cattle buried in a pit at Coygan Camp in Carmarthenshire, and trampled into a land surface at Gwernvale in Powys along with grains of wheat.

Substantial timber buildings have also been found in Wales dating from about 4000 BC. The occupants of these buildings made use of pottery, polished stone axes and a range of flint tools that would have been unfamiliar a few hundred years before. But perhaps most significantly of all, these communities began to build megalithic tombs.

the homes of the tomb builders

Sheep are not native to Britain but were introduced from the Continent around 4000 BC. For those in Wales who lived by hunting, the first encounter with domestic sheep – an animal that was previously unknown and was content to be man's possession – must have been a strange experience.

© The National Museum of Wales (Tony Daly)

The megalithic tombs appear to have been the only structures built in stone at this time. If their builders were to revisit them today, they might be shocked to see them as tourist attractions, but they would still be able to recognize them for what they are. They stand out as monuments of another age, their chambers surviving relatively unchanged as the world alters around them.

Every other structure was made of wood, which is of course degradable, and therefore finding evidence of the homes of the tomb builders has proved an ongoing challenge for archaeologists. Within a hundred years of construction a wooden building would be approaching dilapidation unless refurbished with new timbers and fresh roofing. Eventually, the roof supports would give way and the wall timbers would rot and collapse, until all that was left were the holes in the ground where posts were once set. Then these too would be lost as vegetation reclaimed the land.

For these reasons, although over a hundred megalithic tombs are known in Wales, only a handful of contemporary settlements have been identified, and almost all of these have been discovered by people who were looking for something else at the time.

Of the meagre selection available, the most complete is a settlement at Clegyr Boia, a small hill protruding from the level plain west of St David's in Pembrokeshire. Its name links it with the early medieval Irish chieftain Boia, who supposedly made his home here only to be evicted by St David himself. It was first dug in 1902 by Sabine Baring Gould, composer of the hymn *Onward Christian Soldiers* and a man who was probably more interested in discovering Boia than in the early settlement he stumbled upon. Although he published his work, it was only in 1943 when Audrey Williams excavated the site that its importance was fully appreciated.

During her work, Audrey Williams revealed two structures that were probably houses. One, an arrangement of stakeholes associated with a scatter of occupation debris, seems precariously close to the edge of the steep hill and appears to be an unlikely place to choose to live. The other is set in a more sheltered location. As well as recovering the ground plans of these two structures, Williams also revealed a very large quantity of pottery. These sherds suggest the remains of household cooking and serving vessels, and their quantity argues for substantial occupation at Clegyr Boia. This latter point is also supported by the discovery of a midden containing more broken pottery, limpet shells and burnt soil, as well as a pit in which fires had been lit. It has also been argued that a stone wall that surrounds the hilltop might date back to this period, although this is far from certain.

There are three tombs within a few kilometres of this settlement, all on the rough land of St David's Head. It is possible that the inhabitants of Clegyr Boia placed their dead in this marginal location to separate them from the rich farmlands adjoining their homes, but the frustrating reality is that no certain link exists between the two. It is equally likely that the tombs post-date occupation at Clegyr Boia by hundreds of years and were linked to other, as yet undiscovered, settlements. At present there is no way of resolving this uncertainty.

A more substantial building was discovered in 1967 during excavation of a large area of land at Llandegai, near Bangor, while developing land for an industrial estate. The main features of this site were two large enclosures that might date from the time of the tomb builders or not long after and an early medieval cemetery. Dug through by one of the enclosure ditches were lines of postholes and timber slots from a 6 metre-wide by 13 metre-long house built around 3700 BC. Found with this ground plan were part of a polished stone axe and pottery of the same type as was found at Clegyr Boia. It would seem likely that this was the homestead of a family of farmers – a view supported by the discovery of many similar sites in Ireland and across Britain.

There is a tomb within an hour's walk of the house at Llandegai, but, once again, it is impossible to be certain whether the same people were responsible for building both monuments. This is a perennial problem where a settlement has been discovered in reasonable proximity to a tomb. The only circumstance in which it has been overcome is when the tomb and settlement are physically linked. This was the case at Gwernvale, a megalithic tomb near Crickhowell which was excavated by the Clwyd-Powys Archaeological Trust in the 1970s. Here, a series of postholes was discovered, partially covered by the later tomb. The postholes presumably belong to the ground plan of a building like the one discovered at Llandegai. But even this is not certain, as not all buildings need have been houses. Perhaps the tomb builders at Gwernvale were not building over an abandoned home, but over a building with a ceremonial function. The same doubt exists at Trostrey in Monmouthshire, where buildings have been found associated with a burial monument.

Surprisingly, these examples are the best yet to be found in Wales – the tomb builders appear to have hidden themselves very effectively behind their megaliths. The other occupation sites that have been discovered are even harder to interpret, such as one at Redberth in Pembrokeshire, with a scatter of postholes and areas of burning that date to some time after 3900 BC. Here the footprint of a round house can be seen in the scatter, but the remaining plan is ambiguous.

Clusters of pits, sometimes containing fragments of pottery, flint and bone, are another common discovery from this time and examples have been found across Wales, but again the question remains – what were they for? It is possible that they

Five thousand-year-old pits at Llanbedrgoch in Anglesey. Features like these, dating from the time of the tomb builders, have been found across Wales. The examples shown here contained pottery of a type common in Ireland.

© The National Museum of Wales (Mark Redknap)

The house at Llandegai in Gwynedd, undergoing repairs. (Based on excavated evidence from Llandegai and similar house sites.)

© The National Museum of Wales (Tony Daly)

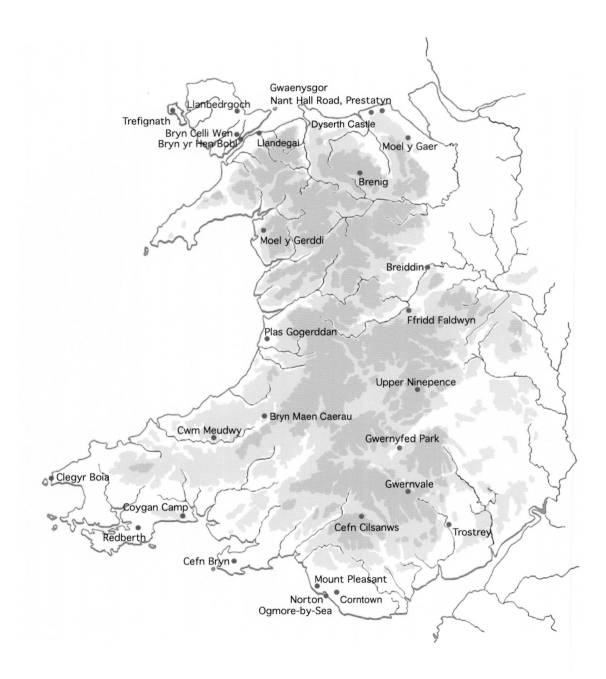

Trefignath

Llanbedrgoch

Gwaenysgor
Nant Hall Road, Prestatyn

Bryn Celli Wen
Bryn yr Hen Bobl

Dyserth Castle

Llandegai

Moel y Gaer

Brenig

Moel y Gerddi

Breiddin

Ffridd Faldwyn

Plas Gogerddan

Upper Ninepence

Bryn Maen Caerau

Cwm Meudwy

Gwernyfed Park

Clegyr Boia

Gwernvale

Coygan Camp

Cefn Cilsanws

Trostrey

Redberth

Cefn Bryn

Mount Pleasant

Norton
Ogmore-by-Sea

Corntown

were dug adjacent to settlements that have since been ploughed away, or that they were intended as a way of disposing of household rubbish; or even that they were dug and filled as part of a ritual by people who lived far away.

In Ireland, the situation is very different, thanks partly to a surge in developer-funded archaeology in recent years. Here, over fifty houses have been identified to go with well over a thousand megalithic tombs found across the country. They suggest that in the years following 4000 BC the country was steadily filled with farmsteads. Indeed, in County Mayo the stone-walled outlines of fields have even been discovered beneath a peat bog.

While early farmsteads remain elusive in Wales, there is adequate proof of agriculture. As well as the domestic animal bones and cereal grains, an equally important environmental record shows an increase in the number of areas of woodland cleared, presumably in order to make room for crops and settlements. The evidence for these clearances comes from pollen trapped in peat bogs. By sampling layers of peat and recording the changes in the types of pollen present through time, it is possible to reconstruct past vegetation cover. For example, sampling of a peat bog near a prehistoric settlement at Moel y Gerddi in Gwynedd revealed a sharp decline in the local woodland not long after 3900 BC, presumably as a result of deliberate clearance. This was followed by re-growth of the woodland and a further clearance episode before 3300 BC.

the builders themselves

The distribution of sites in Wales that are known to have been occupied between 4000 BC and 3000 BC.

© The National Museum of Wales (Tony Daly)

Although the homes of the tomb builders are hard to identify, the people themselves are well known from their bones. The majority of megalithic tombs were used repeatedly, with new bodies added to the bone pile over many years.

Megalithic tombs were not the only places that people were buried at this time: many bodies were also placed in caves. But the 6,000 years that have intervened between their death and the present day have not been kind to their remains and have presented many obstacles to their survival.

The first obstacle is environmental, since not all types of soil are equally suited to preserving bone. Acidic soils, which are common throughout Wales, eat into the calcium of bones, breaking them down until there is just a stain of phosphate-rich earth to mark where they once lay. In contrast, alkaline soils, such as those common above limestone bedrock, are kinder to human remains, and in these conditions bones can survive for millennia.

The second obstacle to the survival of the tomb builders' remains has been the inquisitiveness of later generations. There are many nineteenth-century accounts of local people being encouraged to dig inside megalithic chambers in search of treasure. It is extremely unlikely that they ever discovered anything to reward their efforts, but in some cases chambers were completely dug out and their contents scattered. This is not only a recent phenomenon: in several cases Iron Age beads or Roman pottery have been found in burial chambers, suggesting that curiosity about megalithic tombs has been a long-lived feature of Wales's history. It is unfortunate that burial places that were so carefully constructed to survive the rigour of the years should have acted as a beacon for later generations of treasure seekers, antiquarians and archaeologists.

The majority of surviving human remains have been discovered in tombs in the south-east and north-west of Wales. But calculating the number of bodies placed in each one is not always an easy task, since the majority of collections have been badly weathered and jumbled over the millennia. The figures that follow, for the population of each tomb, should therefore be read as approximations.

In south-east Wales, the remains of at least six individuals were found at both Penywyrlod[1] and Thornwell Farm, although neither site was fully excavated. Detailed study by Mick Wysocki and Alasdair Whittle of the remains from Pipton, Ty-Isaf,

[1]   There are two tombs in Wales named Penywyrlod, both are in Powys. The first, noted here, is near Talgarth, the second near Llanigon. Throughout this book, where no location is indicated, the tomb referred to is that near Talgarth.

THE LANGUAGE OF THE TOMB BUILDERS

A language barrier is one of the major difficulties in the study of megalithic tombs. Not knowing the names of the tomb builders encourages us to think of them as distant and mysterious, whereas knowing the name of a castle builder, or the saint to which a church is dedicated, helps to make the monuments of later times seem more normal.

But in recent years one theory has been proposed which, if correct, might allow us to claim some common ground with these remote people. Since the eighteenth century, scholars have noted the similarities that exist between many of the modern languages of Europe and those of southern Asia. For example, in both Welsh and French the word for 'one' is 'un' (although they differ in pronunciation), in German it is 'ein' and in Bengali 'eka'. Hundreds of other similarities exist, all of which suggest that these languages developed from a common root – a language that has been named Proto-Indo-European. Proto-Indo-European was spoken by a community that migrated out across Europe and into India, its original language changing and splitting into evolved forms as the group fragmented.

Where and when these Indo-European speakers began their migrations is a matter of great debate, the traditional view being that this common language – the root of both English and Welsh – did not arrive in Britain until after 1000 BC. However, a more radical theory, developed by Colin Renfrew of Cambridge University, which has found support from statistical analysis and genetic profiling, argues that Indo-European had arrived in Britain by 4000 BC, perhaps with the tomb builders themselves.

Whether this theory will stand the test of time has yet to be seen, but if it does it raises the possibility that at least a handful of the words we use are related to those spoken by the tomb builders.

Tinkinswood and Parc le Breos Cwm, all tombs that have been more thoroughly excavated, have shown that at these sites at least eleven, seventeen, twenty-four and forty individuals were interred respectively. Archaeological records provide information about other populations in tombs in this area. In 1888, members of the Monmouthshire and Caerleon Antiquarian Association excavated human bones from the tomb of Heston Brake, and in the early 1920s the amateur archaeologist C. E. Vulliamy dug at several tombs in the Black Mountains of south-east Wales. Vulliamy records that at Ffostyll South 'about 600 bones, teeth, and fragments were collected and removed for examination. The remains were those of not fewer than nine

individuals.' He went on to discover further human remains in a subsequent excavation. At neighbouring Ffostyll North, another six or seven were found, while at Little Lodge and Penywyrlod (Llanigon), he uncovered eight and twelve individuals respectively.

In north Wales, the conditions for preservation are generally less favourable. Areas of limestone outcrop are less widespread and soils are generally acidic. Even so, four sites in particular are known to have produced large assemblages of human remains: Pant y Saer, Lligwy and Bryn yr Hen Bobl in Anglesey, and a significant collection at Tyddyn Bleiddyn in Denbighshire.

Pant y Saer was initially despoiled in 1874 by treasure seekers who found five lower jaws, one of which was taken to a nearby farmhouse. Many more bones were found when antiquarian diggers returned to the tomb. The site was next excavated by W. Lindsay Scott, a well-known archaeologist who was knighted following his service in the Air Ministry during the Second World War. He reported the discovery of over forty bodies at Pant y Saer, which he described in some detail. Lligwy was excavated in 1909 by E. Neil Baynes, another respected archaeologist, and the remains of more than thirty bodies were discovered. Bryn yr Hen Bobl was excavated with great care by the Secretary of the Royal Commission on Ancient and Historical Monuments in Wales and Monmouthshire, W. J. Hemp. Working over six seasons from 1929, he discovered the bones of around twenty individuals of all ages and both sexes.

Tyddyn Bleiddyn was dug in 1869 and 1871 by the famous cave excavator William Boyd Dawkins and associates. Their work revealed the remains of many individuals of all ages and many of these were analysed by George Busk, one of the leading anatomists of his day. But subsequent treatment of these bodies has not served later generations of archaeologists, or indeed the memory of the tomb builders themselves, well. Some of the bones were reburied in a churchyard, as the maid-servants were afraid to sleep in the house where they were stored. Fortunately, at least one skull and many small bones from the tomb were passed to the National Museum of Wales. A further two skulls at the Museum might also be from Tyddyn Bleiddyn, but it is impossible to be certain, as no record of their provenance exists. Three more skulls from the tomb are in the collections of the Duckworth Laboratory in Cambridge, to which they were donated at some point in the late nineteenth or early twentieth century. The other human remains excavated by Dawkins are now missing.

The muddling, separation and loss of remains from Tyddyn Bleiddyn offers an important lesson regarding the care that must be exercised if excavated remains are to continue to be kept intact. However, even the most rigorous management of remains cannot ensure their preservation in all circumstances, as demonstrated by events at London's Royal College of Surgeons: in 1941, in a single night of wartime bombing, the majority of bones then known from Wales's megalithic tombs were destroyed.

In the early years of the twentieth century, the Hunterian Museum at the College provided a focus for the study of the human skeleton. Its collections, developed by the physical anthropologist Arthur Keith, were global in extent and covered both archaeological and modern remains. They were so valuable that the College could rightly claim in 1920 that 'Through tradition [and] the force of circumstances ... it has come about that our Museum contains the most extensive and valuable collection of Racial Crania and skeletons in the British Empire. It is one of the standard collections of the world.'

Keith was generous in extending his expertise and that of his staff in the identification of human remains, and bones from Bryn yr Hen Bobl, the two tombs at Ffostyll, Little Lodge, Lligwy, Pant y Saer, Penywyrlod (Llanigon), Tinkinswood and possibly other tombs in Wales were sent to him for study. Many of these collections were subsequently donated to the Hunterian Museum.

The storage conditions at the Hunterian Museum were as good as anywhere else in Britain at the time, and the College had an impressive catalogue of its collections. Staff were also alert to external pressures that might jeopardize their collections; for example, during the First World War, collections were moved into basements in case of attack by enemy aircraft. During the Second World War, these measures were taken even further and basements were strengthened against air raids. But on the night of 10 May 1941, over 500 German aircraft attacked London in the last great air raid of the Blitz. The Museum was hit, as the College's annual report for that year describes: 'A heavy high explosive bomb struck Room V and the subjacent War Museum and store-rooms, utterly demolishing them …. Incendiary bombs completely gutted Room III, the Historical and Mummy Rooms …The Osteological Series (Human) sustained particularly selective loss'.

In a single night, and more than five thousand years after their burial, the remains of dozens of Wales's megalith builders were destroyed by shock waves and fire. The bones that survived were muddled in the debris, allowing only a few to be identified, rescued and passed to other museums – notably London's Natural History Museum.

Fortunately, not all the human remains excavated before the Second World War were in London at the time of the Blitz. Bones from Tinkinswood and Bryn yr Hen Bobl had been returned to their excavators in 1914 and 1934 respectively. These became part of the collections of the fledgling National Museum of Wales. Some rare nineteenth-century collections that never passed through the hands of the College are those from Parc le Breos Cwm and Heston Brake. Parc le Breos Cwm was excavated in 1869 by John Lubbock, but the human remains found there were reburied in the tomb by the landowner, only to be re-excavated by Richard Atkinson of Cardiff University in 1960-61 and passed to the National Museum of Wales as recently as 2001. Heston Brake was excavated in 1888 by the Monmouthshire and Caerleon Antiquarian Association. This society was one of only a few in Wales to have its own museum at this time, a factor that led to the preservation of the bones until their incorporation into the collections of the National Museum of Wales in 1931.

Apart from these acts of fate, there is one other reason for the poor preservation of human remains in Wales's megalithic tombs. Not all of the bodies were interred as inhumations. Cremation was practised at many sites, with the body being burnt on a pyre. During the cremation process bones split and fracture, breaking down into small pieces that are often too tiny to be identified. This is the cost of cremation to modern

A store room in The Hunterian Museum in London, after the German bombing of 10 May 1941. The intensity of the fire that swept through the room can be seen from the charring on the shelf supports.

Courtesy of The Royal College of Surgeons of England

researchers. However, as a minor compensation, cremation also removes the calcium from human bones, making them far more resistant to attack from acidic soils. Cremated bones have been found at several tombs in north-west Wales, for example Barclodiad y Gawres, Bryn Celli Ddu, Bryn yr Hen Bobl and Din Dryfol. They have also been identified at Carreg Coetan Arthur and Twlc y Filiast, among other sites in the south-west. Cremation was also practised in the south-east, but more rarely.

In total, therefore, the remains of over one hundred people once buried in Wales's megalithic tombs are now preserved in museum collections. Apart from being slightly shorter on average, these people were physically very similar to ourselves. They were certainly not apemen or Neanderthals, and it is very doubtful that they would have matched the modern stereotype of shambling cavemen. The bones that have been preserved show that representatives of all sections of the population were buried in megalithic tombs, regardless of gender or age. At Pant y Saer several foetuses were buried, while at Tinkinswood a newborn baby was interred. At the other end of the age spectrum, the very elderly were buried at Penywyrlod. In all cases, these remains

VIOLENT DEATH

Despite the number of bodies that have survived from the time of the tomb builders, it is very difficult to identify how any particular individual met their death. However, one body from Penywyrlod provides an exception to this rule. Reanalysis by Mick Wysocki in 1999 of the human bone from Penywyrlod revealed that a fragment of flint, presumably the broken end of a knife or arrowhead, was embedded in a rib bone. Furthermore, there was no evidence that the bone had begun to heal, suggesting that whatever violence had been meted out had been fatal. The Penywyrlod bone is the first evidence for violence in Wales's history – a dispiriting accolade – but it is not the only contemporary evidence of this type from Britain. Another individual from a tomb in Oxfordshire also has a flint arrowhead embedded in a vertebra, while several other individuals in tombs in southern England appear to have been attacked with blunt instruments leading to skull fractures. Furthermore, at least two enclosures in England appear to have been attacked by bowmen, with hundreds of arrows being found around them. So, it would seem that violence was not just a matter for individuals. It appears that life at the time of the tomb builders carried with it a predictable level of aggression, violence and warfare.

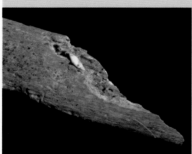 

Left: *A human rib from Penywyrlod, showing the flint tip embedded within it.*
© The National Museum of Wales (Jim Wild)

Right: *A selection of arrowheads. It is very likely that the piece of flint embedded in the body from Penywyrlod was the tip of one of these finely crafted points.*
© The National Museum of Wales (Jim Wild)

were mixed with those of other ages and of both sexes. There is no evidence in these remains for any divisions in society that excluded particular groups from burial or mistreated sections of the population. The differences we can see between the tomb builders and ourselves are likely to have been a consequence of the lives they lived, which were of necessity more physical than our own.

Their lives certainly involved a great deal of hard labour, and while they worked they risked injury. The people buried at both Penywyrlod and Tinkinswood had spent a considerable amount of time squatting, resulting in facets developing on their shin

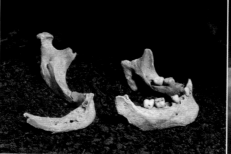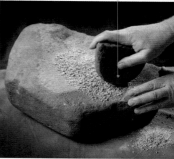

bones. One had damaged his upper arm in a way often associated with the use of a slingshot. Broken bones were also in evidence: at Parc le Breos Cwm, one individual had evidently broken his left elbow, and although the break healed, it did not do so cleanly and his movement would probably have been restricted. Another individual had a bony spur on an upper arm bone, which might have been the product of a heavy fall. A broken forearm is also recorded on an individual at Ty-Isaf.

Disease was as prevalent then as it is now, with the additional problem that there was no modern medicine to alleviate its effects. One individual from Penywyrlod shows signs of an inflammatory scalp disorder, which led to pitting of the skull surface. At Lligwy, an individual is reported to have had a growth that might be evidence of cancer, although this has not been confirmed by modern analysis.

This litany of hardship suggests that life for the tomb builders was 'nasty brutish and short' [2], but there is ample evidence that it was not always so. A woman was buried at Penywyrlod who had lost almost all of her teeth long before her death, yet still she lived to old age. Detailed study of growth marks (Harris lines) on the bones of children from Parc le Breos Cwm indicate that food was regularly available. Indeed, these people seem to have suffered less from certain afflictions than we do today. For example, there is little evidence of tooth decay, presumably as a result of the lack of sugars in the diet. However, a dental problem that was prevalent was the grinding down of teeth by the quantity of grit that was consumed along with food . In some cases, for example at Tinkinswood, this might have been the reason for several cases of abscesses.

Reconstructing the diet of the tomb builders was, until recently, an unsatisfactory business. It was known that the construction of tombs coincided with

2   Thomas Hobbes, Leviathan, 1651

Left: *An upper arm bone from Parc le Breos Cwm on Gower, with a marked bony spur half way along its length. This might have been caused by healing after the overlying muscle was torn; in an undamaged bone the surface would be smooth.*
© The National Museum of Wales (Jim Wild)

Centre: *The jaw of an old woman from Penywyrlod (left), shown beside that of a younger individual. The old woman lost her teeth before she died, and their sockets had been resorbed into the bone, leaving her jaw thin and fragile.*
© The National Museum of Wales (Jim Wild)

Right: *A grinding slab found at Gwernvale in Powys. Slabs like this one were used to grind cereal grains to make flour. Grit from the slab was incorporated into the flour at this stage and contributed to the high levels of wear on teeth.*
© The National Museum of Wales (Jim Wild)

LONG SKULLS AND ANCIENT DNA

In the middle of the nineteenth century, archaeologists began noticing recurring traits in the shape of the skulls they recovered from megalithic tombs and other archaeological sites. In crude terms, it was observed that people who inhabited Wales at the time of the tomb building had long skulls, while those of later people were more rounded. It appeared that the tomb builders' 'racial type' had been identified. In Wales, one researcher working in the 1910s and early 1920s, H. J. Fleure of Aberystwyth University, attempted to find these skull shapes within the modern population in an effort to prove that the descendants of the tomb builders lived on. Fleure's work involved measuring the skulls and recording the family histories of 2,500 people, with the decision being made 'to concentrate upon the simpler folk, as the more leisured classes are nearly everywhere of very mixed descent'. Fleure's conclusion was that people with suitably shaped skulls 'persist in abundance in Wales and are especially characteristic of the inland valleys around certain moorlands which are their immemorial homes.' It is fair to say that Fleure's conclusion that some of Wales's population was unchanged since the Stone Age did not meet with widespread acceptance. Today, his results

the appearance of domestic plants and animals in Wales, and the obvious inference was that this was the food that was consumed. Indeed, animal bones are known from several tombs, and equipment for grinding cereals has been found at others. But questions still remained: was meat the major food of the tomb builders, or did plants form the bulk of their diet? And for those who lived within reach of the sea, what percentage of their diet was seafood?

The application of stable isotope analysis by the archaeologists Rick Schulting and Mike Richards has begun to provide answers to these questions. This technique examines isotopes of nitrogen and carbon in bone collagen. The proportion of each

would be discounted on several grounds, not least the sheer unlikelihood of communities surviving unaltered for over 5,000 years despite the known migrations of population that have occurred in the intervening centuries.

Although more recent research by Neil Brodie of Cambridge University has confirmed that the builders of megaliths generally had long skulls, a greater understanding of these ancient populations is likely to be gained in future from the study of DNA. On the one hand there is the possibility, should science advance sufficiently, that the DNA within the bones of the tomb builders might itself be analysed. On the other, techniques that allow the profiling of the DNA of modern populations might also be used to determine the DNA profile of the population of Britain at the time the tombs were being built.

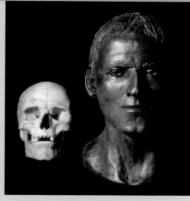

One of the men buried at Penywyrlod. This reconstruction, based on a skull from the tomb, presents us with an unexpectedly sensitive face.

© The National Museum of Wales (Jim Wild)

depends on the types of food the deceased person consumed to gain protein, whether it be from plants, animals or marine foods. Within the context of tombs in Wales, the technique has, to date, only been applied to the remains from Parc le Breos Cwm, which is set within a few kilometres of the sea. Here, there was no evidence of marine foods in the diet of the people in the tomb, and very little evidence for the consumption of plant foods. It seems that the population relied to a great extent on animal foodstuffs (meat, milk and possibly blood). Similar results have been obtained from contemporary burials in caves. In each case, the population seems to have ignored the resources of the sea and turned instead to the land.

2

the world
of the living

Based on the evidence of settlements that have been excavated across the British Isles, it seems likely that people at this time lived in small communities with no villages, nor regional capitals. For parts of the year it is possible that families lived with little contact with others beyond their close kin, cut off from their neighbours by the wild woods around them. This could not, however, have been the case all year round. If people had no contact with other groups, archaeologists today would not find the same pottery style being used from one end of the British Isles to the other, nor would they find common types of megalith. At a very basic level, without contact with other groups no single family would have been able to sustain a level of genetic diversity to prevent them becoming inbred – they must have had contact with other groups.

meeting places

In England the causewayed enclosure is one class of site that is commonly interpreted as a focus for such inter-group activity. These enclosures consist of circuits of ditches, broken at intervals by causeways that allowed access to the interior of the monument. Some causewayed enclosures have several ditch circuits, while others have just one, but they would all have appeared as a tamed clearing in a landscape that was still mostly wooded. Excavation at these sites has produced a great variety of evidence, much of it indicative of feasting and communal activities. For example, at Windmill Hill in Wiltshire and Hambledon Hill in Dorset archaeologists found large numbers of slaughtered animals and significant amounts of pottery. Although many other activities are known to have occurred at causewayed enclosures – for example, exposure of the dead, burial, and occasionally occupation – it seems likely that as a group these types of monuments served to bring disparate communities together.

The quest for similar sites in Wales has a long history. In 1929, at about the time causewayed enclosures were becoming widely recognized in England, the

archaeologist W. J. Hemp thought he had found one at Dinas near Llanidloes in Powys. This suggestion was never proved however, and the hunt for the gathering places of the tomb builders has continued. The first possible success in the hunt came in 1990, when archaeologists from Southampton University revealed a layer of staining at the base of a small test pit they were digging at Bryn Celli Wen in Anglesey. More extensive excavation revealed two lines of ditches running broadly parallel to one another. Within one of these ditch segments was found a polished flint axe, while another held a broken megalith apparently deliberately tumbled into one of the ditches and smashed. It appeared that Wales's first causewayed enclosure had been found, albeit at a site that did not have all of the features of the southern English form. A more classic example was discovered at Norton in the Vale of Glamorgan in 1984 during a study of air photographs that had been taken by the Ordnance Survey, and further aerial photography in 1996 provided greater definition and allowed an outline plan to be produced. This shows all the features of a typical causewayed enclosure, with roughly circular ditch circuits interrupted by numerous causeways.

Another example might also have been discovered at Banc Du in Pembrokeshire in 2003 – work continues at this site to determine its date. However, two causewayed enclosures of classic form do not seem like a reasonable result for over seventy years of searching, and it therefore seems likely that in most of Wales there were other kinds of places at which the tomb builders gathered.

It is possible that they used natural features in the landscape as the focus for their gatherings: hill tops, river confluences and lakes that people could return to year after year. These landscape features might have been sufficiently well-known in their own

Meeting at Gwaenysgor in Flintshire. The results of excavations on this hilltop raise the possibility that it was once used as a meeting place. It certainly commands a dramatic location,

40 the world of the living

overlooking the low-
lying land to the
north, and would
have been well
known to
communities living
beneath it.

© The National Museum
of Wales (Tony Daly)

right, without the added definition of a bank and ditch. It is possible that many of the
pits noted previously are the remains left behind by such gatherings. The same might
be said of general scatters of flint and pottery found on hills such as the Breiddin and
Ffridd Faldwyn (both in Powys) – both of which became the site of Iron Age hillforts
over three thousand years later. A scatter of material was also recovered beneath the
site of Dyserth Castle, while a large assemblage was excavated from a nearby hilltop
at Gwaenysgor – a site that affords impressive views out across the Vale of Clwyd. It is
certainly possible that all of these were the sites of meeting places.

the axe trade

Perhaps the clearest indication that people maintained contacts beyond their immediate neighbourhoods is provided by the distribution of an otherwise mundane tool, the stone axe. Stone axes were rarely used prior to the introduction of agriculture into Britain, but from 4000 BC they became common, suggesting that the felling of trees

and the working of wood had become a major part of life. Production of a stone axe-head needed a large piece of relatively high quality material that could be sharpened and would stay sharp. This meant something other than the locally available pebble flint, which was only suitable for the making of smaller knives and scrapers.

The distribution of flint axe-heads makes it clear that communities in Wales were acquiring these tools from southern England, where good quality flint was readily available. Quite how these imports were obtained is not clear. It is possible that they were passed on from one community to another and that the person in south Wales who used the tool never met the person who had made it. Even so, the axe trade is evidence that Wales's tomb builders were aware that they were part of a much wider world. Clearer evidence of individuals travelling long distances, linking communities in

different areas, is provided by the distribution of another type of stone axe-head, this time made of a type of stone only found in Cornwall. Axe-heads of this type were rarer in Wales, but they are generally found in coastal areas, implying that mariners voyaged between the two areas. Support for the view that communities in Wales and Cornwall were linked in a social network is also offered by the distribution of one style of megalith common to both areas (see p.58).

The traffic in stone axe-heads was not entirely one-way, since Wales also possesses abundant rocks well-suited to the manufacture of axe-heads. In north Wales in

Distribution of exports from the axe factory at Graig Lwyd (left) and the Preseli Hills (right).

© The National Museum of Wales

particular, areas of quarrying have been identified from which blocks of stone were extracted to be turned into axe-heads. At Graig Lwyd on Penmaenmawr, people noticed that a particular kind of rock (augite granophyre) was especially suitable. Excavations have since located piles of waste flakes created when the blocks of stone were roughly worked into shape. The finished axes themselves were distributed across Wales and into southern and eastern England, and as they were passed from person to person and moved further from Graig Lwyd they presumably gained value as exotic items made of a foreign and unfamiliar stone, as well as being simple tools. Other types of stone that were exploited for the manufacture of axes have been identified on the Lleyn Peninsula in north Wales and in Pembrokeshire.

The impression gained from all this evidence is of small communities coming together on occasion to meet and hold ceremonies, but always linked by a broader network of loose contacts that bound together wide areas. These links might well explain some of the common features that can be seen in the design of megalithic tombs across Britain, Ireland and even further afield.

different types of tomb

3

F amiliarity with two or three megalithic tombs might give the impression that they are haphazard in design. As their raw materials are unworked stone, no two are precisely alike. However, when one reviews the shape of two or three hundred tombs from across the British Isles, clear patterns emerge that allow us to make some comments on the cultural affinities of their builders.

The presence of architectural 'types' is immensely important to archaeologists when trying to classify the tombs into groups and to explore the cultural similarities displayed by their creators, whether deliberately or subconsciously. Several clear types have been identified in Wales, each of which has provided insights into the nature of the megalithic world. But many tombs are just too simple to be classified into anything but the broadest group. This is a particular problem in the south-west. Here, there are many small tombs with simple chambers that defy classification, such as King's Quoit in Pembrokeshire and the tombs at Morfa Bychan in Carmarthenshire, which are essentially slabs of rock perched on upright stones.

An equally frustrating problem is the classification of tombs that have been badly damaged. Centuries of stone robbing have almost completely removed the mounds that once covered many megalithic tombs, leaving their chamber stones protruding from the earth like stripped bones and their mounds indistinct. Stone robbing also affects other parts of the tomb, for example, chambers, kerbs or facades. Careful excavation can do much to resurrect the missing features of a site. For example at Pentre Ifan, long considered to be a denuded chamber, W. F. Grimes was able to locate the holes in which the stones of a facade and kerb had once stood. Few sites have been excavated in such detail, and for many damaged sites it is impossible to say a great deal about the classification to which they belong. However, sufficient work has been undertaken to allow particular types of Welsh tomb to be identified, with one of the most fundamental bases for distinction being the shape of the covering cairn, whether round or long.

passage tombs

Megalithic tombs covered by a round mound are generally found in the west of Britain. A common type is the passage tomb. In this style the roofed chamber is normally at the centre of the mound, with access being afforded by the provision of a straight passageway through which visitors walked or crawled, depending on the ceiling height. Passage tombs are best known in Ireland, with the most impressive being the massive tombs at Newgrange and Knowth in the Boyne valley. These tombs can be of enormous proportions. The mound at Newgrange has a diameter of about 80 metres, rises to over 13 metres and contains roughly 43,000 cubic metres of stone. Knowth is a similar size and is surrounded by over seventeen smaller passage tombs.

These giants are just the peaks in a distribution of similar tombs that can be found in northern Scotland, northern and eastern Ireland, west Wales, south-west England, Brittany and the coast of Spain. That this common theme of round mound, central

The passage tomb at Newgrange in Ireland, after reconstruction in the 1960s. This massive monument dwarfs the passage tombs of Wales, but they are linked by form, art and burial rite. In the foreground is part of a pit circle, built around 2000 BC, long after the construction of passage tombs had ended.

© The author

chamber and connecting passage can be found over such a broad area is evidence that there was a degree of communication between the communities along the Atlantic coast of Europe, and that some communities in Wales were part of a broader cultural tradition that looked to the Atlantic shoreline for its inspiration.

Perhaps there was a sea-borne migration. Perhaps the knowledge of passage tomb building was carried by fishermen who sailed up and down the Irish Sea and Atlantic coast in search of a catch. Or perhaps the Atlantic seaboard was just a busy thoroughfare that linked communities who chose to express themselves in a common culture. Much later in history, these same lands were to become the focal point of the Celtic world - a cultural grouping that continues to have meaning today.

In Wales, the passage tomb tradition is best seen at Barclodiad y Gawres and Bryn Celli Ddu in Anglesey. Although both of these sites are heavily restored, they still convey how it must have been to enter one of these tombs, proceeding down the passage into the dark of the chamber, cocooned within the earth. There are other passage tombs in the west of Wales, although these tend to be less well-preserved, with only the surviving passageway indicating the original affinity of their design. In all cases, the scale is trivial when compared to Newgrange or Knowth, and even the impressive Bryn Celli Ddu is only 26 metres in diameter.

More impressive in size than Barclodiad y Gawres or Bryn Celli Ddu is the tomb at Bryn yr Hen Bobl in Anglesey. The broadly circular mound at this site has a diameter of 38 metres and a central chamber, but there was no passage that would allow it to be classified as a passage tomb. Instead, there was a concavity in the side of the mound

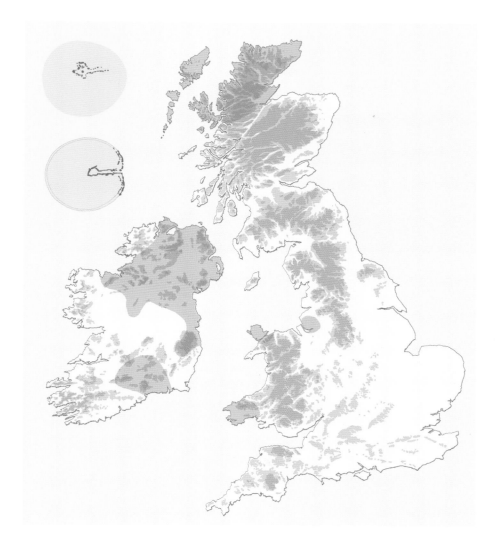

The distribution of passage tombs in Britain and Ireland, with plans of Barclodiad y Gawres (top) and Bryn Celli Ddu (bottom), illustrating the typical round mound and long passage of this type.

(c) The National Museum of Wales (Tony Daly)

that allowed access to the chamber and gave the mound a sort of kidney shape. A similar arrangement can be seen at the smaller tomb of Pant y Saer, also in Anglesey. Perhaps these are local interpretations of the passage tomb tradition: round mound, central chamber but no passage. It is not too surprising that there are local variations when it is considered that megalithic tombs were being built in Wales over several hundred years. Taking into account the extent to which even the most conservative of our more modern building traditions have changed over a similar timespan, it would

Bryn Celli Ddu in Anglesey is one of the most impressive passage tombs in Wales. Unusually, it has a stone circle and the remains of an infilled ditch around its outside - archaeologists continue to debate whether these elements are part of an earlier monument.

© The National Museum of Wales (Kevin Thomas)

be unrealistic to expect Stone Age builders, working without written plans, to conform to a single design. It is also important to note that all tombs set within round mounds are not necessarily part of the passage tomb tradition, as will be seen.

Turning to tombs with rectangular mounds, there is ample evidence for variation of design. They can be found all across Britain and Ireland, and within these islands they have a distribution that is far greater than passage tombs. Distinctive regional groups can be identified in the vicinity of the River Severn (Cotswold-Severn tombs), Ireland (court tombs), south-west Scotland (Clyde tombs) and lowland Britain (earthen long barrows). These types of tomb are not found exclusively in these areas nor are they the only types of rectangular mounded tombs that can be identified in the British Isles, but they are the ones of greatest relevance here.

cotswold-severn tombs

Cotswold-Severn tombs were built with trapezoidal cairns (rectangular with one end wider than the other) ranging in size from about 15 metres to over 50 metres in length. The wider end often curves inwards to create a forecourt area that might have served as a focus for ceremony and ritual. The concentration of tombs of this type around Gloucestershire has led to the choice of name Cotswold-Severn, but it is a choice that leaves many tombs in Wales divorced from their neighbours, since the

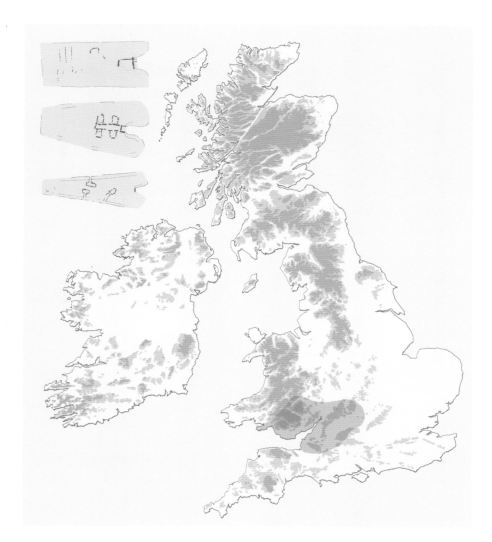

The distribution of Cotswold-Severn tombs, with plans illustrating the three main types: single chamber (Tinkinswood), multiple chambers opening from the forecourt (Parc le Breos Cwm) and multiple side chambers (Gwernvale).

© The National Museum of Wales (Tony Daly)

distribution also extends west into Glamorgan and out to Gower, as well as north into the Black Mountains at the eastern end of the Brecon Beacons. Furthermore, there are more distant tombs that are clearly linked to this tradition, such as Capel Garmon and Tyddyn Bleiddyn in Denbighshire.

The external appearance of Cotswold-Severn tombs is the defining feature of the group, but clear sub-styles can be seen within their cairns. In some cases the chamber opens off the forecourt, and occasionally it is subdivided into separate stalls.

Tinkinswood in the Vale of Glamorgan is a good example of the former instance, while Parc le Breos Cwm on Gower illustrates the latter. Just as frequently, the centre of the forecourt was blocked by a dummy stone, creating the false impression that a chamber lay beyond. In these cases the chambers were accessed from the long sides of the monument. The reasons for these differences are unknown. It is possible that one sub-style grew out of the other, or that each carried different cultural connotations, but at present there is too little dating evidence to know for certain. Apart from the internal differences, the broad similarity in the form of Cotswold-Severn tombs across a wide area does indicate a degree of cultural cohesion among the tomb builders.

The essential form of Cotswold-Severn tombs with their trapezoidal mound and forecourt can be seen in other areas, for example across Ireland and western Scotland. However, in both these areas there is a distinctive regional style to the monument. The builders of court tombs in Ireland placed considerable emphasis on the forecourt, which in some cases was almost entirely enclosed by a stone facade extending from the front of the cairn. The Clyde tombs of Scotland are distinguished by a particular building technique applied within the chambers, which consist of paired slabs overlapping one another and creating a series of box-like compartments. Neither of these specific styles seem to have greatly influenced tomb builders in Wales, although a single tomb in Anglesey, Trefignath, does contain features that would not be out of place in a Clyde tomb. Unsurprisingly, evidence suggesting contact with tomb building communities in Scotland is found in the most northerly part of Wales.

Similarly, it is to be expected that communities on the eastern border of Wales should have been influenced at some time by styles of tomb used in England, most notably the 'earthen long barrow', which is common in southern and eastern Britain. In these areas, slabs of stone and boulders were much rarer and tomb builders either

Left: *Tinkinswood in the Vale of Glamorgan.*
© The National Museum of Wales (Kevin Thomas)

Right: *Capel Garmon in Denbighshire. One of the northernmost tombs to display Cotswold-Severn traits.*
© The National Museum of Wales (The author)

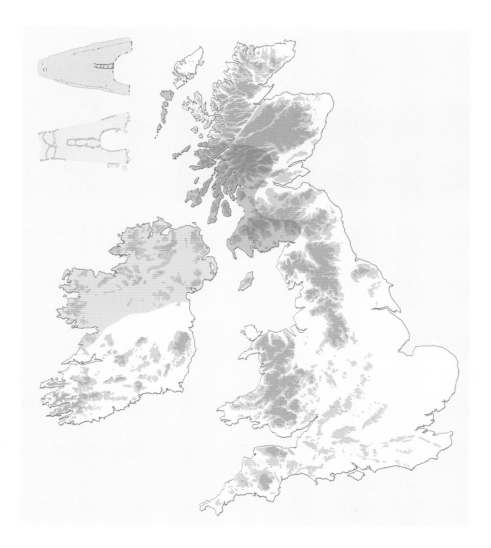

Distribution of Clyde tombs (red) and Court tombs (orange) with plans of the two types.

© The National Museum of Wales (Tony Daly)

had to seal the bodies beneath a mound of earth or place them in wooden chambers that soon rotted away within the barrow. An example of this type of tomb has been excavated by Alex Gibson at Lower Luggy in Powys.

These then are the main styles of rectangular cairned or mounded tombs that can be identified in Wales. As with round cairns, not all tombs with rectangular cairns necessarily fit easily into these categories, for example Twlc y Filiast in Pembrokeshire and Nicholaston on Gower. In the former case, the chamber and forecourt are not

distinctive enough to place the site into a specific category, and in the latter, the single chamber appears to have been sealed within an otherwise featureless rectangular cairn.

So far, the distinction between round mound and rectangular mound has been helpful in subdividing Wales's megalithic tombs. However, there is one tomb type, important to Wales, that defies this simple subdivision: the portal dolmen.

portal dolmens

In Wales, the classic portal dolmen is Pentre Ifan in Pembrokeshire. This has a simple box-like chamber with a massive capstone. Two stones flank the entrance to this chamber, which is in turn sealed by a blocking stone. It is this H-shaped arrangement of stones at the entrance that gives rise to the term 'portal'.

At Pentre Ifan, the chamber is at the end of a rectangular cairn, but elsewhere this is not always the case. In the first phase of building at Dyffryn Ardudwy in Gwynedd, a similar chamber was set within a round cairn. In this case it was clearly the chamber that defined the monument rather than the enclosing cairn or forecourt. Portal dolmens are found throughout Ireland, western and southern Wales and south-west England. The extent of this distribution overlaps with that of several other tomb types. Indeed, with the possible exception of the Black Mountains area, where Cotswold-Severn tombs are dominant, there are no parts of Wales where a single tomb style was employed to the exclusion of all others. For example, in Anglesey, passage tombs were built, as well as tombs influenced by Cotswold-Severn and southern Scottish design. There are also non-descript tombs that defy classification. It

Above left: *Trefignath in Anglesey. This tomb was built in several phases, with the style of the largest chamber suggesting that the builders had links with the Clyde region of Scotland. Behind the tomb is a rock-cut ledge, which might be the remains of a quarry for building material.*

© The National Museum of Wales (The author)

Above right: *Trevethy portal dolmen in Cornwall, showing the jauntily angled capstone that is a feature of many portal dolmens. The skill with which these capstones are balanced is one of the most notable traits of this style of tomb.*

© The author

Right: *Pentre Ifan in Pembrokeshire.*

© The National Museum of Wales (Kevin Thomas)

The distribution of portal dolmens in the British Isles.

© The National Museum of Wales (Tony Daly)

could be argued that this variety is just a reflection of different communities migrating through the island, each one building their own style of tomb before being superseded by another. Although the several hundred years of tomb building in Wales would certainly allow for this argument, there is not sufficient dating evidence to justify it. It is more likely that communities in Anglesey, and elsewhere in Wales, were simply following fashions of tomb design and burial rite that ebbed and flowed alongside inter-regional alliances and trading links.

CERRIG Y GOF

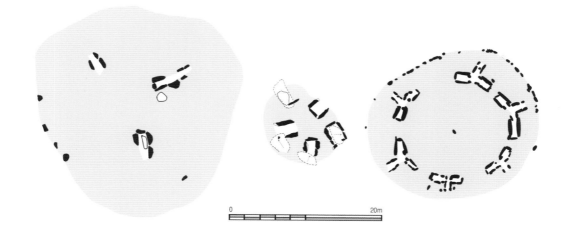

Cairnderry in Scotland (left), Cerrig y Gof in Pembrokeshire (centre) and the Mull Hill Circle on the Isle of Man (right).
© The National Museum of Wales (Tony Daly)

Not every tomb belongs to a particular type, and not all tombs with a similar shape need necessarily share a common ancestry. The tomb at Cerrig y Gof in Pembrokeshire demonstrates this.

Cerrig y Gof consists of five separate chambers arranged in a rough circle within a round cairn. It was excavated some time before 1810 by the antiquarian Richard Fenton, though he made no significant discoveries there. In form it is unique in Wales and there are few parallels elsewhere. Indeed, the tombs that have repeatedly surfaced in the archaeological literature as possible parallels for Cerrig y Gof are the Mull Hill Circle on the Isle of Man and a style of tomb in south-west Scotland of which Cairnderry is a good example. The former is over 200km away, the latter over 300km.

All have the same radial arrangement of chambers and are set close to the Irish Sea.

Are these sufficient grounds to suggest that communities in these areas were sharing the plans of their burial monuments? Perhaps, but it is also possible that three entirely separate communities in Wales, the Isle of Man and Scotland, all fuelled by a culture of tomb building, decided independently to build a form of monument that was unique in their experience.

choosing a location

4

Above:
A reconstruction of Din Dryfol in Anglesey, showing the tomb sometime after its completion.

© The National Museum of Wales (Jackie Chadwick)

Right: *A model with a painted backdrop, showing the construction of Pipton in Powys. Probably produced in the 1950s with the guidance of the tomb's excavator, Hubert Savory. Although largely*

The reasons why megalithic tombs were built at specific points in the landscape are often difficult to discover. In some cases, a particular landscape feature has clearly influenced the builders: for example, the tomb of Din Dryfol in Anglesey was built on a natural platform halfway up the side of the cliff-like face of a small hill. This hill serves as a dramatic backdrop, framing the site very precisely, and there are similar attempts to use outcrops as backdrops in south-west Wales. Another use of a landscape feature can be seen at Mynydd Troed, a Cotswold-Severn tomb carefully sited on a saddle-back ridge between the mountains of Mynydd Llangorse and Mynydd Troed in the Black Mountains. This ridge is an obvious crossing point for people travelling east to west across the mountains, and the tomb must have been visible to all. By contrast, Twlc y Filiast in Carmarthenshire and Parc le Breos Cwm on Gower are situated at the bottom of river valleys. Their locations did not afford the tombs long views, but they ensured that they would have been unmissable by any travellers using the valleys as a routeway.

Seafarers approaching the coast would also have caught sight of tombs, since many were built on promontories with open views of the sea. For example, Barclodiad y Gawres in Anglesey and King's Quoit in Pembrokeshire both command sea views and are situated beside good beaches at which boats could have been grounded. Those mariners who landed on these beaches would have been left in no doubt that this part of the land was already owned. The reverse argument is that tombs were not built so they could be seen by passers-by, but so that the dead within them could continue to watch events in the lands of the living. Unfortunately, too little is known about the nature of belief at this time to choose between these two possibilities.

Another logic for the siting of tombs was the choice of locations with historical significance for the builders, for example on the sites of abandoned settlements. Gwernvale, where a megalithic tomb was built over an earlier occupation area and timber building, is one instance of this. Similar instances can also be noted in England and Ireland. It is possible that by building over old settlements an attempt was being made to link the dead with their ancestors who had once lived on the land. Certainly, the site at Gwernvale had been visited and used intermittently for more than five thousand years previously.

Other tombs were constructed in locations where burial monuments already existed. Examples are Carneddau Hengwm in Gwynedd, Ffostyll in Powys and Sweyne's Howe on Gower, where two tombs can be seen side by side, or at Morfa Bychan, where as many as four tombs might once have been present. Sometimes even building a new monument in close proximity to an existing tomb seems not to have been enough for the tomb builders and an existing monument was enlarged and enhanced instead. It has been suggested that several tombs in Wales were developed in this way, for example at Dyffryn Ardudwy, Trefignath, and possibly Pipton and Ty-Isaf (see p.79), although it should be noted that some archaeologists are less certain that the construction phases at these sites were separated by significantly long periods.

Visibility, historical significance and proximity to other tombs are all clear reasons for building tombs in specific locations. However, another consideration that might have overridden many of these in the minds of the builders could simply have been the availability of suitable raw materials.

the availability of materials

It was noted earlier that in many parts of southern and eastern Britain the lack of suitable stone precluded the building of megalithic tombs and less durable timber monuments were built instead. This was not a problem faced by people in Wales, where surface outcrops of suitable stone are readily accessible in most areas. In many instances, tomb builders located their tombs within easy reach of glacial boulders or outcrops and minimised the huge resources that would be involved in moving massive stones over a distance.

There are no instances in Wales where it can be demonstrated that megaliths were

Left: *The view from Mynydd Troed in Powys. This tomb is perfectly situated to catch the eye of anyone walking up Cwm Sorgwm.*

© The National Museum of Wales (Kevin Thomas)

Right: *Lligwy in Anglesey.*

© The National Museum of Wales (Kevin Thomas)

carried great distances to build a tomb at a specific location. Indeed, there is only one example of transportation of megaliths in the whole prehistory of Wales, and this occurred several hundred years after the construction of the last megalithic tomb. The transportation of the Preseli bluestones from Wales to Wiltshire for the building of Stonehenge was the remarkable exception to the evidence that construction involving megaliths was usually carried out near the source of raw materials.

In some cases, the tomb builders were content to lever a glacial boulder out of the earth and to prop it up above the hole from which it came. This seems to have been the case on Cefn Bryn, a high ridge running along the Gower Peninsula. Over eighteen thousand years ago, a massive boulder was carried to this hilltop by the spread of Ice Age glaciers, and then dropped when those same ice sheets melted away. This boulder was left occupying a superb location overlooking Llanrhidian Sands and the mountains of south Wales, a fact that was no doubt appreciated by the tomb builders who levered it out of the earth and propped it into place with a series of upright stones to form a chamber now known as Arthur's Stone. Here, it seems that it was the presence of the boulder that dictated the location of the tomb, rather than the location of the tomb being decided first and the necessary raw materials dragged with great effort to the chosen spot. A similar sequence of events might have taken place at Carreg Samson and at Pentre Ifan in Pembrokeshire, where a pit found beneath the chamber of the tomb might represent the original location of the loose slab of rock that now forms the capstone.

Evidence of another economical building technique that was reliant on the availability of suitable materials can be seen in areas where the natural bedrock was exposed at the surface and easily split into large slabs. At Glyn in Anglesey a slab was prised out of the bedrock and then propped on one side, creating a lean-to that served as a tomb. A similar approach might have been used at Benllech, Lligwy and Pant y

Saer (all in Anglesey), although in these cases the raised slab was propped and enclosed in a more sophisticated manner.

A number of other tombs are located within easy reach of a supply of boulders or quarry stone that could be used to form their large covering cairns. For example, Tinkinswood in the Vale of Glamorgan is built in an area littered with large slabs of conglomerate, many of which can still be seen in the fence lines approaching the tomb. Some were incorporated into the cairn without moving them from their original position - a technique also illustrated at Twlc y Filiast in Carmarthenshire, which was built on top of a supply of locally derived boulders and slabs. Gwernvale (Powys), Parc le Breos Cwm (Gower) and Capel Garmon (Conwy), among many others, have cairns composed of quarried stone that was probably derived from adjacent outcrops, while at Trefignath in Anglesey a sandstone quarry was identified just to the west of the site. At several sites, for example Morfa Bychan in Carmarthenshire, tombs were built directly beneath rock outcrops and cliff-lines that would have provided building materials as well as a dramatic location. In some cases, tomb builders used other materials that were close to hand in place of stone, as at Lower Luggy in Powys, where the mound was composed of earth, while at Barclodiad y Gawres in Anglesey, the mound consisted of peat which had probably been cut from a nearby marshy valley.

Whichever material was selected, the construction of a tomb required careful planning of manpower, time and materials. While it cannot be known for certain how these resources were measured by the builders, the evidence suggests that they were keen to minimise the amount of effort their enterprises involved without compromising the ambition of tomb building. Fortunately, in a land as rich in stone as Wales, this still allowed them many opportunities to site tombs at locations that would add both drama and significance to their enterprises.

5

building the tomb

raising the capstone

The most remarkable element of tomb construction is the raising of the capstone. Even today, these massive, floating stones evoke wonder. At Tinkinswood, a 40-tonne capstone measuring 6.5 metres by 4.5 metres was lifted, while at Pentre Ifan, a stone 4.3 metres long by 2.4 metres wide was raised over two metres high. That such feats were undertaken at all, let alone that they have survived aloft for almost 6,000 years, is a credit to Stone Age engineering.

The technology available to these engineers appears basic today, but was obviously sufficient for the task - there is no need to invoke the supernatural. Stones themselves could be used to raise ground levels, provide footings and act as weights. Timber could provide frameworks, levers and ramp surfaces, while ropes of bast (plant fibre) or honeysuckle could secure construction apparatus. The only qualities available then but not so abundant today are experience in using these materials and the expectation that they could be used successfully.

Arthur's Stone on Gower has one of the largest capstones of any tomb in Wales. At some time in the past it split in two. The smaller fallen piece is lying in the foreground on this photograph.

© The National Museum of Wales (Kevin Thomas)

In 1857, the King of Denmark, Frederick VII, entered the debate on how megalithic tombs were built. In a thorough and clearly thought-out paper reprinted in Archaeologia Cambrensis *he discussed two methods by which capstones could have been raised. In the upper illustrations, the chamber is dug out beneath a stone and uprights wedged in place - as has been suggested for Arthur's Stone on Gower. In the lower illustrations, the uprights are positioned first and the capstone raised onto them.*

Courtesy of the Cambrian Archaeological Association

Most attempts to re-enact the raising of large stones have focused on Stonehenge, where 10-tonne lintels were raised almost seven metres above the ground. Richard Atkinson of Cardiff University was one of the first to study seriously the methods that might have been employed, and he identified two main possibilities: either earth or timber ramps had been constructed and the lintels pulled up them, or a crib of wood had been built around the lintels, which were slowly levered up allowing another layer of timbers to be placed beneath them until the right height was reached.

The crib method was tested in 1994 by Julian Richards and Mark Whitby for a television series and was found to be very successful. The ramp method was also found to work, with a team of ninety people raising a lintel 6 metres off the ground in three hours. In another experiment in Czechoslovakia by Pavel Pavel, a system of timbers, ropes and levers was used to raise a five-tonne lintel 3.9 metres using only ten men. Although such experiments do not offer conclusive proof of the way large stones were lifted during tomb construction, they do give some idea of the scale of the operation. Smaller capstones, weighing probably only a few tonnes, were more easily lifted. During the excavation of the passage tomb of Knowth in Ireland, it was found that twelve men were perfectly capable of moving a one-tonne capstone. At

Hazleton in Gloucestershire three archaeologists managed to manhandle the largest half-tonne stone used in the tomb chambers, although it would probably have taken twice as many people to drag the stone to the site in the first place.

Unfortunately, excavation at many of Wales's megalithic tombs has failed to provide clear evidence for the details of the construction method used: only at Capel Garmon did archaeologists discover the remains of holes that might have held posts associated with the building of the chamber. The detail of the building technique is therefore open to conjecture, and the usual assumption is that the chamber uprights were positioned first and the capstone then placed on top. It should be noted, however, that in at least a few cases where the capstone had simply been lifted from its recumbent position, such as at Arthur's Stone, Carreg Samson, Glyn and Lligwy, it is likely that the capstone was raised first and the uprights propped into position beneath it. Experiments undertaken by engineer Cliff Osenton have demonstrated that this construction technique could be very economical in terms of labour.

the walls of the passage and chamber

The upright slabs that form the walls of chambers and passages, and those upon which the capstone sits, appear to have been placed with little preparation: at most tombs these stones were simply placed upright on the ground or set in very shallow sockets. At some excavated sites the remains of a small cairn has been identified, which presumably stopped these loose wall slabs from falling down until the capstone could be lowered, letting its weight fix them in place. Buttressing cairns seem to have been common in south-east Wales, with examples having been identified during excavations at Gwernvale, Penywyrlod, Ty-Isaf, Pipton and Tinkinswood. It is possible that in some cases these buttressing cairns might also have served as ramps up which the capstones could have been levered. The intricacy of balancing one large stone on several irregular uprights left room for error. In several

cases, for example at Capel Garmon, Bryn yr Hen Bobl and Bryn Celli Ddu, the irregular tops of the stones were levelled by layers of drystone walling that the capstone then held in place. Conversely, at sites such as Gwern Einion in Gwynedd, the capstone has been set at a deliberately jaunty angle, as if to defy gravity.

At many tombs in Wales, only the chamber and capstone survive, but at others the remains of a cairn can be identified, sometimes surviving to quite considerable size, and enabling us to work out more about how they were constructed.

drystone walling

As well as their use for levelling the tops of chamber walls, drystone walls were also used as a way of defining the limits and enclosing the bulk of a tomb's surrounding cairn.

Although irregularly shaped stones and boulders can be used to delineate structures,

in order to construct stable and neat drystone walls it is necessary to have access to a supply of stone that can be split into fairly regular slabs or blocks. These can then be arranged in lines raised to the required height. Drystone walling has been found at many well-preserved tombs across Wales, indicating that the technique was widespread. It was presumably also used in many other construction projects such as property boundaries, enclosures and buildings.

At Pipton, two rows of drystone walling were used to create an inner and an outer wall around the cairn. At the foot of the inner wall a layer of chippings was found, which suggests that the workmen had stood at the wall, trimming each stone to fit the required spot. The inner wall was built fairly roughly and more attention was paid to the finish of the outer wall. A similar situation was found at Gwernvale, where the outer wall was made of a finer, more workable stone, leading to an aesthetically pleasing affect. This belt-and-braces approach was common and might have been intended to stop the weight of the cairn from slipping outwards and buckling a single wall. Buckling was evidently a problem, as demonstrated at Penywyrlod, where the cairn appears to have overwhelmed both revetment walls at the rear of the monument. To prevent any further slippage, a trench was dug parallel to the rear of the cairn and a series of upright stones were bedded into it as a buffer. The dangers of cairn slump could also explain the fact that at Tinkinswood, where only a single wall was identified surrounding the cairn, that wall was 1.5 metres thick.

In north Wales, drystone walls have been identified around the north cairn of Carneddau Hengwm and around the forecourt at Dyffryn Ardudwy, while at Bryn yr Hen Bobl in Anglesey an outer wall, still surviving to a height of 2.4 metres, encircled the cairn. This had a well-built outer face and was constructed sloping inwards to assist its stability, while its inner face was bonded into the cairn, so it would seem that both were raised together. Unlike the raising of capstones, drystone walling is still a living craft, practised throughout the north and west of Britain. Indeed, it is likely that the techniques used today have much in common with those used by the builders of megalithic tombs.

A reconstruction of drystone walling at Parc le Breos Cwm on Gower.

© The National Museum of Wales (Tony Daly)

building the cairn

The construction of the cairn is likely to have involved more than simply manhandling stones into a haphazard pile. Unfortunately, details of cairn construction have generally only been identified in south-east Wales.

The first stage in cairn construction might have been the setting out of the plan using marker stones. These would have fixed the alignment of the cairn while the chambers were being built. Possible examples have been identified at Penywyrlod, Ty-Isaf, Pipton and Pentre Ifan. At Tinkinswood, there is also evidence for the sequence in which the cairn was built. During the excavations, several lines of stones were found inside the cairn, which compartmentalized the interior. It is possible that these were intended to add stability to the structure by preventing any slippage from one compartment to the others, although they do not appear substantial enough for this purpose. Alternatively, it has been argued that this practice reflects a division of labour among the builders, with families taking charge of filling their own compartment. Similar internal walls have been identified at Penywyrlod and possibly at Din Dryfol, as well as at several sites in England, indicating that the practice was commonplace. More substantial walls within the round cairn at Bryn yr Hen Bobl might also have served to stabilize the cairn.

The construction of cairns must have been a labour-intensive and repetitive process. In some areas it is likely that surface stones were used (for example at Twlc y Filiast and in the first tomb at Trefignath), while in others the cairn material was quarried specially for the purpose. The tools that were available for these tasks would have consisted of little more than baskets for stone carrying, antler digging sticks for grubbing out suitable stones and the shoulder blades of oxen for shovels. The Irish archaeologist Michael O'Kelly has speculated that cattle might have been used to help shoulder the burden of stone carrying, but unfortunately there is no direct evidence for this. (There is also no direct evidence for the use of the wheel in Britain at this time, although it might have been in use in northern Germany and Poland.)

No one has attempted to calculate how long it would have taken to raise the cairns of any of Wales's tombs: few are complete enough to allow such an analysis to be undertaken convincingly. However, the case of Hazleton in Gloucestershire might provide a suitable guide to the effort involved in building the Cotswold-Severn tombs of south-east Wales. This tomb has a cairn 55 metres long and between 8 and 19 metres wide, rising to perhaps 2.5 metres at its highest point. The excavator of the site, Alan Saville, estimated that this cairn consisted of about 742 cubic metres of quarried material, with the stone brought from two quarries set on either side of it. Based on his estimation of the quantity of cairn material and his calculation of the distance this must have been carried, he believed that it would have taken at least 5,225 hours to build: enough work to occupy a gang of ten people for 65 eight-hour days. This would have been a very significant investment in time, especially when we add the time taken to build the passages and chambers that the tomb contains.

Presumably, the construction time involved in raising the 52 metre-long and almost 3 metre-high cairn at Penywyrlod, the largest Cotswold-Severn tomb in Wales, would have been greater still, although in this instance it is not known how far away the stone quarries were situated.

Why the tomb builders chose to devote so much effort to housing the dead when they could have been caring for the living is a puzzle, but it is likely that the two goals were closely intertwined in their minds. If the dead were not cared for, perhaps the crops would fail, or their neighbours might overwhelm them, or perhaps the dead themselves would seek revenge. With such a mindset the building of a tomb would have been the only sensible thing to do.

multi-phase construction

So far, it has been assumed that the building of tombs was undertaken to a single coherent plan: chambers first, then walling and cairn. In many cases this was probably so, but at several others there is evidence that the sequence of construction was more complex.

In 1938 W. F. Grimes excavated at Ty-Isaf in the Black Mountains. The site was selected because surface indications suggested that it belonged to the Cotswold-Severn group. Since no examples of this type had been scientifically excavated in Wales, it was hoped that it would provide an insight into the structure of these tombs in this region.

At the close of the excavation, Grimes could confirm that the tomb had been built in the Cotswold-Severn style, but he also identified an earlier phase of tomb building that was very different in character. This consisted of a round cairn containing a T-shaped arrangement of chambers linked to the cairn edge by a passageway. This round cairn had been incorporated into the rectangular cairn of the later Cotswold-Severn tomb.

Excavations at Ty-Isaf in 1938 revealed a complex history of construction. This photograph, taken from outside, shows the tomb's first passage leading to the chambers beyond. Later in the tomb's history, the cairn was extended and its orientation changed, leaving this passage facing the rear of the completed structure.

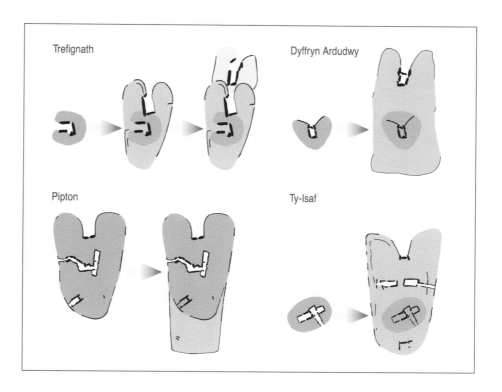

Trefignath

Dyffryn Ardudwy

Pipton

Ty-Isaf

Excavating at Pipton in 1950, Hubert Savory found a related phenomenon. The tail of the cairn had at some point been extended beyond its initial termination, effectively sealing in one of the chambers. The evidence for multiple building phases at Dyffryn Ardudwy and Trefignath has already been described.

It seems likely therefore that many tombs were added to over the years, meaning they were not the result of a single vision; but uncertainty remains as to how much time elapsed between the building of the first phase of a tomb and subsequent additions to it. It could have been years, it could only have been days. Illogical as it might seem, it is possible that, from the outset, the builders of the first phases of Ty-Isaf and Pipton fully intended to conceal these structures within the larger bulk of the Cotswold-Severn tombs. Possibly there was a ritual significance to the act - perhaps the first phase of building sanctified the tomb location, or gave an invisible heart to the finished tomb. Without a detailed series of radiocarbon dates, it might never be possible to settle the question of whether these sites were built to a single vision or added to over a prolonged period.

dealing with
the dead

Understanding how tombs were built is a relatively mechanical affair, dictated largely by resources, logistics and the technology of the time. Understanding how tombs were used is a very different matter, made far more complex by our lack of knowledge of the concerns and priorities of the tomb builders. Before attempting to unravel some of these complexities, it is worth considering the difficulty that the dead would have posed for the living at this time.

Firstly, we can try to work out how many people are likely to have died during the thousand or so years that the tombs were in use by estimating the number of people who lived during this period. It can be assumed that the land could support at least 0.1 person per km^2 - the real figure was certainly much higher. Given that Wales has a land area of 20,778Km^2 and a new generation was born at least every 25 years, a very conservative estimate would be that at least 83,000 people lived in Wales over this period.

Today, only about one hundred tombs survive - nowhere near enough to accommodate such a large population. It is possible that a very large number of tombs have been destroyed in the intervening five millennia, but there is also clear evidence that the tomb builders had more than one way of dealing with their dead.

In 1886-7, William Boyd Dawkins, a well-known explorer and excavator of caves, began work at Gop Cave in Denbighshire. By the time his work was finished, he had uncovered a curious stone-walled chamber set at the back of the cave. Within the chamber were parts of at least fourteen bodies and a range of artefacts that indicated that the bodies dated to the Neolithic - a period that includes the time of the tomb builders. More recently, Rick Schulting of Queen's University Belfast has dated several of these skeletons, with results that confirm Boyd Dawkins's belief. Other studies by Schulting have revealed that this was not an unusual practice, with human remains contemporary with the use of tombs being dated at several Pembrokeshire caves: Nanna's Cave (3370-3030 BC and 3500-3090 BC), Priory Farm Cave (3910-3640 BC), Red Fescue (3770-3530 BC) and Ogof-yr-Benlog (3630-3350 BC). Remains dated between 3950 and 3100 BC have also been found at Spurge Hole on Gower and Little Hoyle in Pembrokeshire. There might be some cases where the deceased were killed by predatory animals and then dragged to the cave; however, this cannot be argued in every instance. For example, the deliberately built burial chamber at Gop Cave is one argument to the contrary, and the presence of seventeen bodies at Little Hoyle is another. It is more likely that these caves were seen as natural tombs, and their passages were a substitute for the megalithic chamber.

However, the combined population of the tombs and caves is still very low for the length of time involved. It might be thought that the missing dead had simply been buried in graves, as happens today, but no such cemeteries or individual graves have been found in Wales. It is also possible that some were thrown into the sea or rivers, but this was hardly practical for many living in inland Wales. The conclusion must therefore be that people at this time also practised burial rites that either did not result in permanent interment, or that involved the destruction of the corpse. One clue to the nature of these alternative burial rites comes from an excavation at Trostrey in Monmouthshire. Here, Geoff Mein excavated a platform that appears to have once served as a cremation pyre. The remains of this structure are slight and were invisible prior to excavation, raising the possibility that there might be many other cremation platforms waiting to be discovered across Wales. If these were indeed once common then it is possible that the missing dead were simply reduced to a collection of broken cremated bones and ashes to be buried or otherwise disposed of.

In England there are hints of other practices that are likely to be relevant to Wales. At Stoney Middleton in Derbyshire, archaeologists excavating a platform surrounded by a low stone wall discovered hundreds of human teeth and small bones. This, it would seem, was where corpses were once laid out to be cleaned of their flesh by birds and slow decay. The larger bones were then gathered together and taken to another location - possibly for inclusion in a megalithic tomb. The absence of many small bones from burial deposits inside megalithic tombs across Britain suggests that the practice of excarnation, where flesh is removed from the body before burial, may have been common, although it should be borne in mind that small bones also tend to be fragile and are less likely to have survived the millennia than larger, robust ones.

In some parts of the world today, the process of excarnation is filled with symbolism. The decaying body is perceived as socially dangerous, because the spirit of the deceased is neither fully dead nor wholly alive, and is certainly not at peace. By managing the decay through excarnation, the body is assisted into the new and stable state of bone, and through this it becomes both fully dead and safe for the living to handle. It is possible that this was the rationale for excarnation current among the tomb builders, with their objective being to aid the transition of the deceased from recognisable individual to common and anonymous ancestor.

If this practice was adopted in Wales, then it is possible that many groups of bones did not find their way into tombs but were deposited elsewhere, perhaps in sacred places above ground - or even in the home.

This range of evidence makes it clear that megalithic tombs were just one way of disposing of the dead. Many more people were probably cremated or excarnated, their bones then being disposed of in other ways. This then raises the question: why were some people buried in tombs and not others?

As we have seen, young and old, both male and female, were interred in tombs, so

In 1908, workmen at Ifton Quarries in Monmouthshire came upon a fissure in the limestone within which were nine or ten skulls accompanied by other bones. No dating evidence exists to prove that this was a burial place from the time of the megalith builders, but the fact that the cave was used repeatedly in a short space of time is certainly in keeping with the burial rites of these people.

Courtesy of the Cambrian Archaeological Association

it is unlikely that age or sex were grounds for discrimination. There is also no evidence to suggest that society was hierarchical at this time, so there is no reason to believe that burial in a tomb was a matter of class. More likely, tombs were built when society felt they were needed, perhaps as a statement of ownership over land or to mark a change in the order of a community. In which case, who was buried in the tomb was a matter of who happened to die when the tomb was in use

7

funerals and ritual in south-east wales

The majority of evidence for burial rites in this region comes from Cotswold-Severn tombs. The dead in these tombs were all treated in roughly the same way, suggesting a common set of beliefs across this area and into Gloucestershire, Herefordshire, Somerset and neighbouring parts. Here, we look first at the structure and design of the tombs themselves, which hint at their suitability for certain symbolism and rituals. Then, we consider the bones and the way they are placed in the chambers and, lastly, grave goods.

rituals around the cairn

One of the most striking examples of apparent symbolism in the construction of Cotswold-Severn tombs is their orientation length-ways towards the eastern half of the horizon, which results in many facing in the general direction of the rising sun. The end that faces in this direction is often built wider and higher than the 'tail' of the cairn.

The importance of the passage of the sun in many religions is well-known. For example, in ancient Egypt the sun god Re crossed the sky in a barque each day, descending into the underworld in the evening, while in classical Greece Helios served a similar role. Today the rising sun carries with it connotations of rebirth, hope and the triumph over darkness, and it would certainly appear that the rising of the sun was woven into the fabric of the tomb builders' culture.

There are some megalithic tombs in the British Isles that are precisely aligned on recognizable solar events, and these are discussed in the following chapter. But there is no evidence that Cotswold-Severn tombs were built with a slavish desire to face the sun at a specific time of year, rather, it seems that it was the general principle of the rising sun and the eastern horizon that attracted the builders.

The eastern end of most Cotswold-Severn tombs also features a forecourt area. Continuing the theme of solar alignment, the curve of the forecourt might demonstrate the desire to hold the sun's rays as they fall on the tomb throughout the

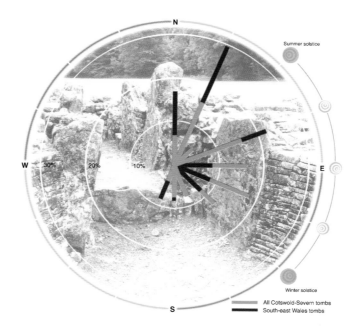

Summer solstice

Winter solstice

All Cotswold-Severn tombs
South-east Wales tombs

Throughout the year, the sun rises at different points along the eastern horizon, swinging from north-east to south-east between summer and winter solstices. Most Cotswold-Severn tombs are aligned somewhere along this arc, although a greater percentage of tombs in Wales are aligned beyond it, to the north or north north-east.

© The National Museum of Wales (Tony Daly)

morning. It is possible that the forecourt was used for ceremonies associated with the burial or commemoration of the dead although, with the exception of a 'ritual deposit' of flint, pottery, bone and possibly stalactite at Parc le Breos Cwm, evidence for this is sparse at Cotswold-Severn tombs in Wales.

At some Cotswold-Severn tombs the chamber is accessed through an opening in the forecourt, for example at Parc le Breos Cwm and Tinkinswood. At others, such as Pipton, Ty-Isaf and Gwernvale, the centre of the forecourt is marked by a false doorway, consisting of a large upright stone that leads the visitor into believing that a passage lies beyond. It is possible that these were intended to confuse would-be tomb robbers, forcing them to waste time opening a doorway to nowhere, although this idea seems better suited to the tombs of Ancient Egypt than to the tombs of Wales. Certainly, the theme of concealment is a recurring one at tombs of this type. Alternatively, and perhaps more realistically, the false doorway might have acted as a visual focus for those who wished to visit the tomb and remember the dead - a gateway for memories, which hinted at the presence of the deceased just beyond, while in fact their spirits were restrained within the heart of the cairn. It could also be

that the false doorway was intended for the dead, not the living, providing a symbolic entrance through which the rays of the morning sun might reach and nourish the entombed bodies. Such a view suggests that tombs were intended as houses for the dead - a place where the ancestors could live on. Some archaeologists have found support for this view in the close similarity between the appearance of long mounded tombs and long houses built in parts of central Europe between 4500-3500 BC. It is possible that tomb builders in Wales had similar thoughts in mind when they combined elements of house architecture with that of their burial places.

The burial chamber is also often concealed at Cotswold-Severn tombs, with the genuine entrance to passages and chambers being hidden, particularly at tombs built in more than one phase. At Pipton, the extension of the rear end of the tomb sealed a chamber within the cairn, making subsequent access to the bodies impossible without dismantling parts of the tomb's structure. In north Wales, secondary building at Dyffryn Ardudwy and tertiary building at Trefignath had the same effect.

The double-skinned walls around tombs like Gwernvale, Penywyrlod, Pipton and Ty-Isaf might also have played a role in concealing tomb chambers. At these sites, the large upright stones of the chambers generally stop at the edge of the inner cairn wall, being continued to the outside of the cairn as a gap in the drystone walling of the outer wall. This gap could be easily filled with rubble and an outer skin of drystone walling, making access to the chamber laborious. Careful excavation at Gwernvale showed this very clearly. Here, it appears that a wall across the entrance to one of the chambers had been built, partially removed and then rebuilt, suggesting that the chamber had been repeatedly accessed and then sealed after each visit.

Above left: *Pipton in Powys, during excavation in 1950. Although these two large stones present a clear focus for the tomb's forecourt, they do not conceal the openings to chambers.*
© The National Museum of Wales

Above right: *Dyffryn Ardudwy in Gwynedd, taken from the entrance of the finished tomb. Behind the massive eastern chamber can be seen the smaller portal dolmen, which was the product of the first phase of construction at the site.*
© The National Museum of Wales (Kevin Thomas)

These visits must have been dark and difficult, as the walls of the passageways
and chambers of megalithic tombs rarely rise sufficiently high to allow a visitor to
walk upright. Instead, they would have had to crouch or crawl on hands and knees. In
addition, the passageways are often quite narrow - too narrow for an individual to
turn around - meaning that most of the natural light would be blocked by the visitor,
who must have carried their own torch or lamp or else felt their way into the
blackness. At many tombs the passageway has kinks and narrowing places, adding to
the discomfort and claustrophobia. Then of course there was the smell of the dead in
such an enclosed space. It might have been considered a privilege to enter the tomb,
but today it seems an unenviable one.

Entering a tomb
© The National Museum
of Wales (Tony Daly)

the burial rite

In entering a chamber the visitor - priest, shaman, elder, mourner or nominee - passed
from the everyday world into an environment that belonged to the dead. Perhaps such
visits were a frequent occurrence, with the bones of the dead being regularly tended;
alternatively, entry might have been closely restricted to times when a new body was
added. In some cases, the remains of dozens of people have been found buried in the
chambers of a single tomb. As it would have been impossible to fit that number of
undecayed bodies into some tombs it is more likely that the bodies were added over a
considerable period, once natural decay had made room for them. At Parc le Breos
Cwm, detailed study of the fragmentary remains found in the chambers showed that

some of the bones had been scavenged by carnivores, probably before their interment, implying their deposition as de-fleshed parcels of bones rather than as bulky bodies.

The idea that the tomb builders valued the spirit of the common ancestor rather than the deceased individual is supported by evidence recovered from other tombs. For example, at Pipton seven separate piles of bone were found in one of the chambers. At first, it might be thought that these constituted the remains of seven bodies, perhaps brought to the chamber as de-fleshed bundles. In fact, the piles are made up of the partial remains of eleven individuals, and each pile contains a mix of bones from different people. It is as though, having broken individuals down into the constituent skeletal parts, an attempt was being made to rebuild the skeleton, albeit without much care being taken to locate the bones of the original person. The same attempt to reconstitute an individual from the common bone pile has been identified at Ty-Isaf, and the stacking of bones by type has been identified at Penywyrlod. These instances suggest that once the bones were deposited in the tomb, specific individuals ceased to be important, although it was sometimes felt necessary to give a human form or at the very least some structure to the mass of the ancestors.

It is possible that the bones of these reconstituted people were not just kept in the tombs, but were brought out into the light of day from time to time and perhaps used in ceremonies. This might explain the very incomplete state of many of the bodies found in tombs, with some individuals only being represented by a handful of bones. However, the potency of these handfuls in the minds of the tomb builders should not be underestimated. At Penywyrlod and Pipton, small collections of human bone were placed underneath rough paving layers in the chambers, possibly indicating that these tombs were sanctified with a token deposit prior to their more active use. At Pipton, this foundation deposit consisted of a tiny fraction of a skeleton, and yet it was sufficient for the task.

Much of the discussion of the burial rite at Wales's Cotswold-Severn tombs has focused on the evidence from just a few sites. Even in combination, this sample is so small that it would be dangerous to assume we have a clear overview of the nature of the burial rite in the tombs of this area. The variety of burial practices current at this time has already been explored, and there are hints that even within a single tomb there was no uniformity of rite. For example, at Tinkinswood and Ty-Isaf cremated remains were added to the bone pile, suggesting that excarnation was not the only route into the tomb chamber. At Parc le Breos Cwm, although, as mentioned, the bones of several individuals found in the chamber had clearly been gnawed by scavengers presumably during excarnation, one contemporary body in the passageway showed no such damage, which could mean that it had been placed in the tomb as a fleshed corpse. Clearly, burial practices were flexible at this time, with the details probably being decided by individual communities.

offerings for the dead

The size and grandeur of the Cotswold-Severn tombs has occasionally encouraged treasure-seekers with the prospect of finding great riches within them. Doubtless, all have been disappointed. In the first place, the tombs were built long before the introduction of metalworking in the British Isles. Consequently, they do not contain gold or silver ornaments, or even rusted iron swords or bronze axes. Their contents are far more humble and spartan, just an occasional pot, a few stone tools and, more rarely, a piece of worked bone. It is possible that other perishable grave goods were offered to the dead, perhaps clothing or wooden objects, food or drink, but of course none of this survives. What little remains does, however, offer clues as to how the living viewed the dead.

The pedestrian nature of the artefacts in tomb chambers is telling in its own way. The broken pots are of the same types as those found on settlement sites. In some

Right: *Stone discs found scattered at Ty-Isaf in Powys.*
© The National Museum of Wales (Jim Wild)

Below left: *Stone scrapers, knives and points are often found in megalithic tombs. It is likely that many other objects were placed in burial chambers with the deceased, but only imperishable materials survive.*
© The National Museum of Wales (Jim Wild)

Below right: *A fragment from a pot found at Dyffryn Ardudwy in Gwynedd. This had had a long life before being placed in the tomb. It had already cracked and its owner had drilled holes close to the break so the two sides could be held together with twine. One of these holes can be seen on the right edge of the fragment.*
© The National Museum of Wales (Jim Wild)

Cat Hole Cave on Gower has been excavated several times, most recently by Charles McBurney of Cambridge University. McBurney's excavations showed that the cave was occupied at the end of the last Ice Age.

© The National Museum of Wales (Kevin Thomas)

cases, they have been broken and then mended, suggesting they were well used before being placed in the tomb. The same can be said of the flint tools, the occasional scraper, knife or broken down axe-head. These were not specially made items, but the stuff of everyday life. If the intention was to offer equipment to the dead for use in an after-life, it appears that tokens were sufficient - there clearly was not enough for each person in the tomb. It is also clear that the range of items placed in the tombs was as variable as the burial rite itself. For example, at Ty-Isaf dozens of individuals were accompanied by fragments of pottery bowls, as well as a flint axe-head, arrowheads (one broken), knives, a bone pin, a stone bead and stone discs.

These latter objects are particularly interesting. Both the bone pin and stone bead appear to be personal accessories, perhaps a clothes pin and a pendant. It is possible that these were worn by the dead before excarnation and were then carried into the tomb along with the bundle of bones. It might also be that they were dropped inadvertently by someone entering the chamber and were lost in the dark.

More enigmatic are the stone discs. Ten of these were found at Ty-Isaf; two came from the chambers and it is possible that at least some of the others were dug out of the chambers by earlier explorers. They are graded in size as though they were intended as a set: their function, however, is wholly unknown. A single stone disc was also found during excavations at Penywyrlod and others have been found in north Wales, implying that these discs were a well-known and recognizable object or tool.

Animal bones are also often discovered in Cotswold-Severn tombs. For example, at Penywyrlod, a pig tooth and the bones of a fox cub, sheep, calf and horse were found. Most of these were not directly associated with the chamber deposits and might simply be the remains of scavenging and scavenged animals. A sheep bone, pierced in three places, is particularly striking. The excavators interpreted this as a possible whistle. If this is true, it is the earliest musical instrument from Wales (see box, right).

Animal bones also found their way into the tomb at Parc le Breos Cwm. These included fragments from at least eight dogs, a cat, red deer, pig, sheep and cattle. Unfortunately, there is not enough information to indicate how these remains came to be there, but one of the roe deer bones was dated to 800-200 BC, indicating that at

WALES'S FIRST MUSICAL INSTRUMENT?

This bone, the broken left femur of a fairly large sheep, 8.5cm long, was found during excavation of one of the chambers at Penywyrlod. Initially, it was not considered to be unusual, but when it was washed three holes were discovered on one side. At first glance it seemed as though the bone was the remains of a whistle, so it was sent to a leading expert on prehistoric instruments, J. V. S. Megaw. His reaction was cautious: while the bone certainly had clear holes,

The Penywyrlod 'whistle'.
© The National Museum of Wales (Jim Wild)

they were rather small, placed tightly together, and rough and unfinished. Nonetheless, he conceded that 'The Penywyrlod bone is the earliest claimant as a musical instrument from the British Isles'.
It is unlikely that this opinion

will ever be categorically proved or disproved. Another possibility is that the broken hole at the end of the bone was made by the tooth of an animal - a dog perhaps. Similarly, the two complete perforations look a little as though they were made by an animal biting down on a dry bone. Indeed, the holes look remarkably rough and unfinished, not what one would expect in an object to which any value was attached, or which had been used for any length of time.

least some of the animal bones entered the tomb long after it had been abandoned. Of more interest is a bone from a badger found at the same site. This was dated to 6640-6410 BC, at least 2,500 years older than the tomb itself. Another large animal bone that could not be identified to a specific species was dated to 11050-10200 BC, the very end of the Ice Age.

It seems likely that these already ancient bones came from Cat Hole Cave, which is a few hundred metres from Parc le Breos Cwm. The bones of any animals that died inside the cave would have been preserved within the silty layers of the cave's floor. Even more intriguingly, the remains of flint tools found at Cat Hole Cave indicate that it was occupied by hunters at the tail end of the Ice Age, raising the possibility that the bone from Parc le Breos Cwm was the discarded remains of a hunter's meal. It would be very interesting to know when and how this bone came to be in the tomb. Did the tomb builders recognize its antiquity and venerate it for this reason? Were corpses excarnated at Cat Hole Cave and the animal bones unwittingly gathered up along with the human remains? Or were the bones incorporated later in the history of activities at Parc le Breos Cwm?

funerals and ritual in north-west wales

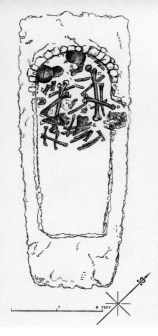

Left: *Pant y Saer in Anglesey, 1874. Several bones had been removed from the tomb prior to the drawing of this plan.*

Courtesy of the Cambrian Archaeological Association

Right: *Pant y Saer in Anglesey.*

© The National Museum of Wales (Kevin Thomas)

The various types of tomb known in north-west Wales have already been discussed: passage tombs, portal dolmens, tombs influenced by southern Scotland, tombs influenced by Cotswold-Severn design and others that defy classification. With such diversity, it might be expected that the funerary rites that took place at tombs were equally variable. Unfortunately, the evidence that would allow archaeologists to explore this possibility is not always well-preserved. However, there are exceptions that offer a glimmer of the traditions that were current, and this discussion begins with one that bears close comparison to the funerary rites described for south-east Wales.

The tomb at Pant y Saer in Anglesey consists of a rock-cut chamber within a kidney-shaped mound. The chamber has been excavated several times, revealing a large quantity of human remains deposited as inhumations rather than cremations.

Once again, there would not have been enough room in the chamber to allow all of the bodies - over forty of them - to have been interred at the same time, so the site must have been used over a long period. Unfortunately, it is unclear whether the jumble of bones found was a result of de-fleshed bones being interred in heaps or of bodies placed in the tomb and allowed to rot before being cleared aside when a new corpse was brought in. One observation that can be made is that there were more long bones in the tomb than there were skulls. It is possible that this is a result of disturbance by treasure seekers, who might have taken the bones they recognized, but it might also be that the dry bones were brought out for ceremonies and sometimes not returned - as has been suggested for tombs in the south-east.

The range of artefacts found at Pant y Saer is also very similar to those described for tombs in south-east Wales - fragments of pottery bowls, flint arrowheads (mostly broken), a scraper and two of the enigmatic stone discs described previously, reinforcing the idea that these were the remains of a common object or tool, but adding nothing to our understanding of their purpose. A bone point and a worked fragment of antler were also found. These scant remains appear insufficient for the number of bodies in the tomb, suggesting that the community that built and filled Pant y Saer was not leaving the items to accompany individuals, but as offerings to the people of the tomb as a group. Similar finds were also discovered at Lligwy along with a large quantity of inhumed remains, although the evidence with which to disentangle the burial rite at this site is even less complete.

Bryn yr Hen Bobl

The site that offers the most complete snapshot of funerary practice in north-west Wales is Bryn yr Hen Bobl. This tomb does not fit easily into a specific category: it consists of a round cairn with a central chamber accessed from a forecourt. Adjacent to the cairn is a low, raised terrace-like feature, 99 metres long and of uncertain function. In the forecourt were three large hearths, implying that fire played a prominent role in the rituals associated with death and remembrance. The excavator at Bryn yr Hen Bobl, W. J. Hemp, described a second chamber at the site, adjacent to the first, but this had already been ruined by the time of his dig in 1929.

Bones from at least fifteen people were found in the remaining chamber at Bryn yr Hen Bobl. This chamber was closed by a single slab perforated by two holes between 16 and 23 centimetres in diameter. The upper part of the slab has broken off, although it seems reasonable to assume that the two holes would have formed circular portholes into the chamber beyond. This closing slab was firmly bedded, raising the

Left: *Within the chamber of Bryn yr Hen Bobl, 'The hill of the old people', in Anglesey. Before the slab was broken, these circular openings were probably the only way to pass material into the tomb.*

© The National Museum of Wales (Tony Daly)

possibility that de-fleshed bones were simply passed through the holes and dropped, the chamber itself being sealed to the living. How bones were placed in the now-destroyed second chamber is unclear.

Arthur Keith of the Royal College of Surgeons of England, who first examined the bones found in the surviving chamber, observed one he believed to have been deliberately cut, suggesting human sacrifice and cannibalism. The deliberate de-fleshing of bodies has not been identified at any other sites in Wales, but it has been identified in England. For example, a collarbone found at West Tump, a Cotswold-Severn tomb in Gloucestershire, had a series of cut marks at locations along the bone that seem to indicate a deliberate attempt to cut the head from the body, and the dismemberment of corpses has been recorded by Mick Wysocki at Coldrum in Kent and Eyford in Gloucestershire. However, these cut marks might have been inflicted as a means of speeding the de-fleshing of the corpse, rather than waiting for decay to do the work.

Barclodiad y Gawres

Other funerary rituals are in evidence at the passage tomb at Barclodiad y Gawres, excavated in 1952-3 by Glyn Daniel and T. G. E. Powell, where the chambers are set at the end of a straight passage. Carved into the stone walls on either side are curving and zigzagging lines, spirals and diamond-shapes, all shimmering as their shadows change in the torch-light. Entering the central chamber, three side chambers can be seen: one ahead, and one each to the left and right. In the right-hand chamber, which had at some time been sealed off from the centre, the cremated bones of two people were found, their bones spread thinly across the floor. Mixed in with their remains were a few sheep bones and fragments of a pin made from antler, all burnt. This combination suggests that animal meat was burnt along with the bodies (although the sheep bones might be later) and, if the pin was used to fasten clothing, that the

From left to right, bone pins from Lligwy, Ty-Isaf, Tinkinswood, Barclodiad y Gawres (3 pieces) and Bryn yr Hen Bobl. These might have been worn by the dead when they were placed in the tomb, or they could have been offerings. The examples from Barclodiad y Gawres are burnt, suggesting they were worn when the dead of this tomb were cremated.

© The National Museum of Wales (Jim Wild)

bodies were still clothed when they were cremated. Bone pins, toggles and beads are a common find in passage tombs in Ireland, making it seem likely that clothing the bodies was a normal practice. The other side chambers had been disturbed by treasure-seekers, and only flecks of cremated bone remained.

The central chamber might have been used for ceremonies and it was certainly large enough to hold several people at a time. In its centre, the excavators discovered a hearth containing the tiny bones of wrasse, eel, whiting, frog, toad, grass snake and small rodents. This strange assortment conjures images of witches gathered around a cauldron, but the excavators suggest a sequence of events. First, a wood fire was lit, presumably filling the confined chamber with smoke. When this had died down, a stew containing the animal bones was poured over the embers and the fire was then quenched with pebbles, earth and shells. (The excavators also thought that the remains could be from the faeces of an otter, but they dismissed this on the grounds that it would be very unlikely for an otter to have such a wide variety of animals in its stomach at one time.)

The choice of animals in this offering appears strange in the extreme. Some might have been viewed as edible, for example the eel, but others are very unlikely to have been eaten or indeed to have served any useful purpose. The evidence would be easier to accept and explain had the stew contained the meat of more obviously prestigious animals like cattle, sheep or deer, but the choice of amphibians and reptiles makes this ritual completely inexplicable. It also appears to have been unique to the community at Barclodiad y Gawres. The style of art carved in the walls of this tomb, and the practice of cremation burial are, however, far more common.

Bryn Celli Ddu

Only 18 kilometres from Barclodiad y Gawres is Bryn Celli Ddu, another passage tomb that was fully excavated in the 1920s. This time the carvings in the tomb were more restrained, being confined to just a single spiral on a stone in the chamber. Also in the chamber was found a 1.75-metre tall smoothed stone pillar that is similar to pillars found in passage tombs in Ireland and a possible example found near the chamber entrance at Barclodiad y Gawres. One view is that the Bryn Celli Ddu pillar might have been intended as a phallic symbol - an interpretation that casts an interesting light on the rituals of death that took place within the tomb - but even with the addition of the stone pillar, the artwork within the chamber and passageway is notably sparse.

Beneath the tomb, on top of a pit set just behind the chamber, lay the most impressive single carved stone yet found in Wales. The curving lines on this 1.5-metre tall slab run across both faces in a continuous swirl, suggesting that it was originally meant to be viewed as an upright, approachable from all sides. How then did it come to be placed over its pit? On the one hand, it could have belonged to an earlier monument, which was erased through the construction of the passage tomb, or it might have been buried at the heart of the tomb as a way of sanctifying the land before it was used. Curiously, the pit over which the stone lay was not entirely empty. Its base had been hardened by fire and a burnt bone and a human earbone were placed within it. The pit had then been filled with a mix of sand, gravel and clay. The meaning of this is lost to us, although it should be noted that the earbone, which is a durable part of the skeleton, might be all that survives of a larger bone deposit that has since decayed away.

This style of art is a common feature of passage tombs in Ireland and further south into Brittany, Spain and Portugal, indicating close links between the communities of the Atlantic seaboard. In Wales's tombs it is concealed within the chambers, implying that it was only intended to be viewed by those involved in the burial ritual. It has been suggested that its curves, swirls and zigzags were attempts to depict images seen in trance-like states, further hinting at the nature of the burial rites that took place within the chamber.

At some sites in Ireland the carvings are enclosed within the chamber, as they are in Wales, reinforcing the idea that this was an art for the privileged few, but this is not the case everywhere. At the great passage tombs of Knowth, Newgrange and at Loughcrew, the decoration also appears on the kerbstones around the cairn where it could be seen by anyone passing by. The details of this art style also varied between regions. In Britain and Ireland, it is largely abstract. In Brittany, a few symbols such as axes and bows can be identified, while in Spain and Portugal human figures occur as well as abstract designs. Sometimes the art of this latter region survives in painted form as well as carvings, raising the possibility that the passage tombs of Wales were once brightly painted, although the relatively damp climate of Wales will have ensured that such traces have long since disappeared.

While art is an obvious aspect of the funerary ritual at Barclodiad y Gawres and at Bryn Celli Ddu, it is harder to draw any conclusions from the paucity of human remains in these tombs. Parallels with the burial rite at passage tombs in Ireland would indicate that the excavators should have found many cremations within their chambers. For example, at least sixty-five individuals were interred at Fourknocks; at the Mound of the Hostages in Tara a 40-centimetre-deep layer of cremated bone was found in the central compartment, while cremated bone littered the chamber floors in some of the well-preserved passage tombs of the Carrowkeel cemetery. When compared with this sort of evidence from tombs in the same tradition, it seems likely that the lack of human remains recovered during careful excavation at Barclodiad y Gawres and Bryn Celli Ddu is a consequence of disturbance by treasure seekers clearing the chambers and scattering their contents. Nonetheless, there is a possibility that the passage tombs of Wales were used as much for ritual as for burial.

The pattern stone from Bryn Celli Ddu in Anglesey.

Sir Norman Lockyer (1836-1920) was an eminent astronomer whose discoveries and accomplishments included the identification of the previously unknown element Helium in the sun's spectrum, the founding of the renowned international journal *Nature* and contributing to the establishment of London's Science Museum.

In 1906, he added the study of astronomical alignments at megalithic monuments to this diverse curriculum vitae, with the publication of the book *Stonehenge and other British stone monuments*. Two years later, he visited Anglesey to determine whether any of its megalithic tombs had been orientated so that the sun, or any other prominent star, would shine into their chambers on particular days of the year. After careful fieldwork, he concluded that Anglesey's tombs were variously aligned on the summer solstice, the winter solstice, the start or end of the growing year or the Pleiades. He was so excited by his findings that in 1909 he published a second edition of his book, in which he wrote:

Before the astronomical study of [cromlechs] was commenced a very few years ago, if we accepted the available records, the cromlechs were all directed helter-skelter, their sight-lines were without any meaning, and no astronomical or practical use was served by them ... A comparatively few observations have sufficed to show the absurd inaccuracy of these views; for full light we may be content to wait for the authoritative inquiries now happily commenced.

Unfortunately, the full light never came and Lockyer's work was largely ignored, principally because it can be very difficult to be precise as to what part of a tomb an alignment should be drawn from: where would the observer have stood? Where

Other evidence for ritual at these two particular passage tombs must inevitably focus on the summer solstice alignment of Bryn Celli Ddu. To build Bryn Celli Ddu with so careful an alignment must have needed considerable planning. At a practical level, the phenomenon of mid-summer's day must have been well-known, at least to someone in the community, and the orientation of the tomb to the sunrise must have been pegged out on a clear midsummer's morning before building work could begin. More importantly, in linking the midsummer sunrise to the community's burial place, it appears that the tomb builders believed that the dead continued to play a part in the annual cycle of life. Perhaps at this time of year the tomb was opened and the light allowed to flood in, revitalising the ancestors. Perhaps new cremations were

OF MEGALITHIC TOMBS

would they have looked? Without this precision, it is possible to argue for many spurious alignments simply by picking suitable stones in a tomb and lining them up with others. A flavour of this problem can be gained at Lligwy, which Lockyer calculated as being aligned on Arcturus or Capella (the 4th and 6th brightest stars in the night sky), while other observers believed it had an equinoctial alignment.

The only tomb in Anglesey where there is any hope of certainty in this regard is Bryn Celli Ddu. Lockyer calculated that the alignment of the passage at this tomb would allow the sun to shine into the chamber at midsummer sunrise. Lockyer's calculations on this point were correct (although there is now a house on the horizon that makes it difficult to see the sun at the precise time of its rising). Despite the uncertainty that surrounds much of Lockyer's other work in Wales, this discovery stands as an important contribution to the study of Wales's megalithic tombs. In making it, he rediscovered the sophistication of the builders of Bryn Celli Ddu.

Bryn Celli Ddu in Anglesey, on the midsummer solstice.
© The National Museum of Wales (The author)

added at this time, with the sun's rays easing the passage of the deceased into the tomb. Or perhaps the alignment served a role in sanctifying the tomb during its construction, making it a fit place for the dead to reside.

There are several broadly contemporary monuments in Britain which were also built with solar alignments, although all of these mark dawn in midwinter. The Dorset Cursus, an earthwork almost 10 kilometres long, is aligned so that the sun shines down its length on the shortest day of the year. The interior of Maes Howe, a passage tomb on Orkney, is illuminated by the sun on the same day, as is Newgrange in Ireland. Here, the light from the rising sun passes through a stone box above the entranceway, down a 19-metre passage and illuminates the chamber beyond.

9

funerals and ritual in south-west wales

The dramatic size and daringly balanced capstones of many tombs in south-west Wales suggest that the very act of construction was one steeped in ritual and tradition. This was not just an attempt to build a stone box, but rather an endeavour to outdo the earth itself, by the raising of an artificial hill. But the tombs themselves give us little evidence for what rituals might then have been performed. Only four tombs in south-west Wales offer any substantial clues: Pentre Ifan, Carreg Coetan Arthur, Carreg Samson and Twlc y Filiast.

Pentre Ifan

Pentre Ifan is a portal dolmen, its chamber being set at the southern end of a long, rectangular cairn. The closing slab of the chamber formed the centre stone in a curving forecourt. This arrangement is reminiscent of the Cotswold-Severn tombs described earlier, and it seems likely that the forecourt was used for rituals associated with the dead. But, whereas the chambers at Cotswold-Severn tombs were designed to be re-opened for the insertion of new bodies, this would not have been possible at Pentre Ifan. The closing slab must have been put in place before lowering the capstone, and removing the closing slab would have meant dismantling the chamber itself.

How then were human remains placed inside? Unfortunately, excavations at the tomb in the 1930s and 1950s did not provide an answer; only charcoal and a few pot sherds were found in the chamber. If bone had ever been present, it had either been destroyed by acidic soils or removed by earlier explorers. Today, the cairn around the Pentre Ifan chamber is very low, presumably as a result of systematic robbing of the stone for building. The question of how high it was originally has important implications for the type of burial rites that could have been easily carried out.

Until recently, it has been assumed that the cairn at Pentre Ifan was originally high enough to cover the capstone completely. This would have made it impossible for whole bodies to be passed into the chamber without dismantling part of the cairn around it. Alternatively, handfuls of dry or cremated bone could have been deposited

Carreg Coetan Arthur in Newport, Pembrokeshire.

© The National Museum of Wales (Kevin Thomas)

in the chamber by reaching through the narrow gaps between the closing slab and side walls, but it would not have been easy to arrange and rearrange the bones within the chamber using only these small openings.

However, if this were not the case and the original cairn only rose a metre or so above the ground, delineating the area around the chamber but not concealing it, then it would also have been possible for whole bodies to be interred, and for these remains to be repeatedly accessed without the need to dismantle the cairn.

The original appearance of the tomb would have been very different, depending on which hypothesis is preferred. In the first, the chamber was a dark and inaccessible place, the closing slab its only visible element. In the second, the entire chamber would have been visible, with the capstone poised on its elegant upright stones above a fringing cairn.

At Carreg Coetan Arthur, Carreg Samson and Twlc y Filiast, small quantities of burnt bone have been discovered, indicating that cremation was practised in south-west Wales. It is possible that inhumation was also practised at these and other sites, but the soil conditions in this region are generally unsuitable for the preservation of unburnt bone and so make it impossible to tell. One observation that can be made for the many other tombs in the south-west of Wales is that the single chambers are generally small, making it unlikely that whole bodies were ever interred within them - few chambers could have held more than a single crouched body.

Unfortunately, the amount of existing evidence for funerary ritual in this region is relatively small, either due to over-enthusiastic and unskilled excavation in the nineteenth century or to the possibility that the tomb builders in this area buried fewer people in each tomb and placed fewer grave goods with them.

Pentre Ifan in Pembrokeshire, some time after its abandonment.

© The National Museum of Wales (Jackie Chadwick)

10

after the
tomb builders

Dating the construction of a tomb is now relatively straightforward. Charcoal or bone sealed beneath the cairn can be radiocarbon dated, providing a date *after* which the tomb must have been built. Using such evidence, it has been determined that Gwernvale was built after 4000 BC and Carreg Coetan Arthur after 3500 BC.

By radiocarbon dating bodies from the tomb chambers it is possible to calculate how long the tomb continued to serve as a burial place. But to achieve this, a large number of individuals from each tomb must be radiocarbon dated in order to be sure of capturing the full timespan over which the tomb was used. Unfortunately, dating every single body is beyond the budgets of most excavators, so inferences must be made from samples taken from only a few of the tombs' occupants. This leads to problems in interpreting the results, as radiocarbon dates only give a rough idea of when a person died, sometimes to within as much as two or three hundred years. Furthermore, combining these dates to give a timespan for the use of a tomb is not straightforward. The most complete dating programme undertaken in Wales has been carried out at Parc le Breos Cwm, and this indicates that the tomb could have been in use for as long as 800 years from 3800 BC onwards - or for as little as 300 years. Dating at Penywyrlod could also be used to indicate a long span of use for the tomb, perhaps as much as 900 years from 4000 BC. Further research is needed to find out which timespan is correct but, in support of the shorter, Alasdair Whittle of Cardiff University has acquired a series of dates from Tinkinswood that suggest the tomb was in use for a comparatively short time around 3700 BC. What is evident is that tombs were used throughout the fourth millennium BC.

It is likely that some tombs were built and used quite late in this period, for example Barclodiad y Gawres and Bryn Celli Ddu. These two passage tombs have not been carbon-dated, but they are very similar in form to tombs in Ireland that were built after 3400 BC. Styles of pottery found in the chambers of Trefignath and Lligwy also indicate that these tombs were still being visited after 3400 BC and 3000 BC respectively. Work by Rick Schulting on bones from Bryn yr Hen Bobl has also shown that this tomb was in use at a similar date.

closing the tombs

While it is possible to date when the tombs were built and when they were in use, it is much harder to prove when they stopped being used, except where the event was marked in some way. Across Wales, tomb building and use declined from about 3000 BC. The tombs containing new styles of ceramics are certainly in a minority after this date and, if the radiocarbon evidence is substantial enough to be relied on, few bodies were added to tombs from this time.

However, many tombs were not just abandoned and left to decline on their own: several appear to have been deliberately sealed. We have already seen how some small tombs were probably sealed by the addition of a second phase of tomb building in front of them, for example at Dyffryn Ardudwy and Trefignath. But there is also a more general, and final, phenomenon.

At the Cotswold-Severn tomb of Gwernvale, between 3650 and 2880 BC, pits were dug in front of the entrance to one of the chambers and flint and pottery, either as offerings or simply the residue of a meal or household waste, were placed in the pits. Not long after these pits were used, unstable parts of the cairn walling were raked down, concealing the chamber entrances and the sides of the tomb. New stone was also carried to the site to complete the task. There is evidence that similar 'blocking material' was also dumped in the forecourt. The result was a featureless mound, with the drystone walling, chamber entrance and probably the forecourt all lost inside. To the excavator, Bill Britnell, it appeared that the owners of the tomb were deliberately emphasising the antiquity of the site, accelerating the weathering that had no doubt been affecting it since its construction.

Similar evidence has been recovered at other tombs in south-east Wales: at Penywyrlod, where the forecourt had apparently been deliberately filled and at Pipton, where the sides of the tomb were also covered by carefully laid stones. In north Wales, during excavations at Trefignath, Chris Smith found that stone had been piled against the side of the cairn as well as in the forecourt. W. J. Hemp encountered similar phenomena in digging at Capel Garmon, Bryn Celli Ddu and Bryn yr Hen Bobl, and

W. F. Grimes found carefully piled stones within the forecourt of Pentre Ifan. These latter cases are particularly interesting, as they show that the closing of tombs did not just occur at Cotswold-Severn tombs, but also at tombs of other traditions, including passage tombs and portal dolmens.

Some of this blocking, particularly of passageways, was possibly regularly undertaken after each burial to keep out intruders or vermin, but the filling of the forecourts and concealment of the cairn flanks imply a general and widespread act of closure. Some slight evidence survives to indicate with what ceremony these acts were undertaken. The pits at Gwernvale have already been noted; at Bryn Celli Ddu, cremated bone was placed in the blocking of the passageway and fires were lit on top of the incomplete forecourt blocking. Perhaps many tombs were built with the expectation that they would only be used for a limited time, perhaps one or two generations, after which they would be blocked. In this case, tomb blocking would have been a staggered affair across the British Isles. But it is also possible that the closing of the tombs was an abrupt and widespread activity prompted by a new cultural order that sought to react against the old ways.

The abandonment of the tomb building tradition was the end of an era. It was a significant event, but it is still not possible to provide a definitive explanation for it. At least part of the answer might simply lie in the length of time over which the tradition existed, since it is clear that in the course of this millennia other aspects of the tomb builders' lives had begun to change.

new traditions

The world of the megalithic builders was, in large part, based on small social groups, albeit ones with well developed regional trade networks and the ability to cluster around international building traditions. A little after 3000 BC, this world seems to have undergone a significant change. In Wales, this change is best illustrated in the archaeology

A timber enclosure in the Walton Basin, Powys, built around 2700 BC. This massive enclosure typifies the new traditions that followed the age of the tomb builders.

© The National Museum of Wales (Tony Daly)

of the Walton Basin in Powys, midway between Llandrindod Wells and Hereford.

Excavations in this area by Alex Gibson have revealed a long history of settlement, some of it predating the tomb builders. Much of this early evidence conforms to the image of a landscape occupied by small social groups, but then, between 2800 and 2500 BC, two enclosures were built. The larger is roughly circular and covers about 34 hectares, has a circumference of 2.35 kilometres and required around 1,410 large tree trunks to form its perimeter wall. Despite intensive study of aerial photographs and investigation using advanced geophysical equipment, no traces of buildings have been found inside this enclosure, although several large pits were revealed. As a result, it is impossible to say with any certainty what people were doing within such a massive enclosure. Possibly it was a tribal gathering point, perhaps it held cattle or perhaps religious rituals were staged there. It is also worth noting that the Walton Basin itself is a location of strategic significance for the control of the surrounding area - it was reused as such by the Roman army during their campaigns to pacify local tribes in the 1st century AD.

Perhaps the most important point to be drawn from the Walton Basin enclosures is that, by 2700 BC, parts of Wales were able to marshal very substantial workforces for centralized projects on a scale not seen in any previous age. The implication seems to be that communities were organizing themselves into larger units, whether these were tribes, clans or just loose affiliations.

Similar evidence exists from this date across the British Isles. For example, there are massive bank and ditch enclosures in southern England, substantial palisaded enclosures in southern Scotland and large circles delineated by timbers, earth or pits in Ireland. It is possible that major building works like these did not impact greatly on the daily lives of communities in Wales - much as the forts of the Romans or the towns of the middle ages might not have greatly affected life in more distant rural areas - but there is certainly evidence that daily life was shifting.

From about 3400 BC pottery styles had been changing, and finely produced and subtly decorated bowls gave way to coarse bowls with haphazard decoration. The style of pottery in common use changed again around 3000 BC, when flat-bottomed jars

decorated with motifs including incised lines and chevrons were introduced. Change even affected the ordinary stone tools that people used in their daily lives, with increasing elaboration of scrapers and knives and the introduction of new types of arrowhead. Whether these changes were a consequence of the building of the massive enclosures, or whether the reverse is true, is impossible to say.

Perhaps most importantly, from around 3300 BC, there is evidence that people were being buried in graves cut into the earth or rock. Between 3350 and 2750 BC, a body was buried at Trelystan; another, buried between 3350 and 2910 BC, has been discovered at Four Crosses and a third (3330-2620 BC) at Sarn-y-bryn-Caled. The act of burial in a grave is final. There is no simple way of revisiting the bones of the deceased, as there is if they are interred in tombs. In addition, the body in the grave could not easily be joined by others at a later date. This new burial rite appears to have had more to do with venerating the individual than in joining them with their ancestors, though in itself individual burial need not indicate the end of tomb use since, as has been seen, other burial traditions had co-existed with megalithic burial for hundreds of years. Nonetheless, the rise of single burials and the end of megalithic tombs do seem broadly to coincide. In combination, the building of massive enclosures and the spread of single burial suggest that the world was moving on, and the cultural connotations of the old tomb traditions could not be adjusted to fit into the new way of life.

With the tombs closed and abandoned they became passive features in the landscape, just humps and bumps in forests, moorland or at the edge of fields. Within a few generations they might have been regarded in much the same way as a ruined chapel or disused village hall is today - part of history, but not of pressing concern to most people. Even so, it seems that their original function as burial places was not forgotten, as later events illustrate.

Types of pottery used in Wales from around 2400-1300 BC. Fragments of pots of these kinds are often found in megalithic tombs – clear evidence of the continued importance of these sites.

© The National Museum of Wales (Jim Wild)

Between 2400 and 1300 BC, long after the closing of the tombs, burial commonly consisted of interring an individual (whether a corpse or cremation) with a ceramic beaker or large urn among other grave goods. Burials with beakers (common from 2400 to 1800 BC) were typically inhumations in stone-lined cists sealed beneath cairns, while those with urns (2200-1300 BC) were generally cremations. Numerous burials were also placed in earlier monuments, including the long-neglected megalithic tombs. Both beakers and urns have been found in the chambers of tombs across Wales, indicating that they were once again being used as burial places - for example, at Barclodiad y Gawres, Bryn yr Hen Bobl, Capel Garmon, Carreg Coetan Arthur, Dyffryn Ardudwy, Ffostyll north, Pant y Saer, Penywyrlod (Llanigon), Tinkinswood, Ty Newydd and Ty-Isaf. Direct evidence for the use of megalithic tombs as burial places in this period comes from radiocarbon dating of bodies at Parc le Breos Cwm where, between 2290 and 2030 BC, a corpse was interred in the passageway, and at Bryn yr Hen Bobl where radiocarbon dating by Rick Schulting has shown that a body was buried between 2300 and 2030 BC.

It seems that, after a period in which tombs were rejected, society had come to terms with them as part of history. It is possible that burial in a megalithic tomb implied that the dead were linked to the ancient owners of the land - the original tomb builders. There might have been status and prestige associated with the act. It is certainly an indication of the continued power of these monuments, hundreds of years after they were apparently abandoned.

Other evidence of the revived importance of tombs can be seen in the presence of curious cup-marked hollows on the chamber stones of Trellyffaint in Pembrokeshire, and at Dyffryn Ardudwy and Bachwen in Gwynedd. These hollows were made by repeated hammering, and are found in groups: at Bachwen, around 110 were found on one megalith. Cup-marks are found throughout Britain, normally carved on slabs of natural stone. They are generally assumed to date to the same period as beaker and urn burial, although a growing body of archaeologists believes that some of these marks date back to the construction of the tombs themselves.

The purpose of these cup marks remains elusive. In the context of the tombs it is

MEGALITH CONSTRUCTION AFTER THE TOMBS

The end of tomb building in Wales was not the end of megalithic construction. Large stones continued to be moved and erected after tomb construction ceased, but from 3000 BC the stones were generally smaller, and the monuments harder still to interpret. It was now the age of standing stones and stone circles.

Standing stones are among the most ambiguous of prehistoric monuments. For the most part they stand in isolation: massive rough monoliths of uncertain purpose. Well over 300 survive in Wales, but they remain difficult to get to grips with for two reasons. First, it is hard to estimate when specific stones were erected, because datable offerings were rarely placed beneath them. Second, there are many reasons why someone might want to raise a standing stone. It might serve a religious role, or act as a boundary or place marker, or it might just function as a scrape against which livestock could rub themselves free of mites.

Harold's Stones in Monmouthshire
© The author

The best that can be offered at present is the view that most standing stones were erected in the thousand years after about 2000 BC.

Stone circles appear, at first glance, to offer more hope of an explanation, but here too they often frustrate. Circles of upright stones were occasionally built when megalithic tombs were common, for example, the circle around Bryn Celli Ddu. But the majority of the eighty or so in Wales date from between about 2500 to 1200 BC. It is possible that they were used for seasonal festivals and

as meeting places; sometimes people were buried within them. Once again, the evidence is slight.

These types of sites are evidence that megalithic construction was not forgotten, but they do not suggest the same majestic grasp of their medium that is demonstrated by the tombs. Gone are the massive capstones and the stone-walled chambers, to be replaced by more mundane and technically simpler constructions. Beyond Wales, megalithic tomb building continued in some areas such as north-east Scotland, Cornwall, the Scilly Isles and across Ireland, but the new styles developed in these areas were not to the liking of the descendants of Wales's tomb builders and were not adopted. However, Wales's stone did continue to make a contribution to megalithic building traditions in one important case: Stonehenge. This monument has a unique relationship to Wales (see p. 128).

possible that they were used to mark an interment, or to signify the importance of the place. Certainly, a convincing case has been made in some parts of Britain that cup-marks were placed at significant points in the landscape.

The reuse of tombs between about 2400 and 1300 BC is evidence of the continued fascination these monuments exerted over our prehistoric ancestors. However, after this time their use as burial places appears to have ceased. Instead, they took on other roles; perhaps they were venerated as the homes of ancestors or old folk, possibly they were feared for the same reasons. Some might have been viewed simply as curiosities, while others were regarded as just an obstacle to farming.

Patchy evidence shows that people continued to visit some tombs. At Trefignath, a radiocarbon date based on charcoal from the eastern chamber indicates that someone had visited the tomb between 400 and 90 BC. The fire could have been lit in an attempt to stay warm in a convenient dry shelter, or as part of religious activities in the age of the druids. Some spindle whorls in the same chamber could also date to the same visit. At Gwernvale, the discovery of a yellow glass bead also indicates a visit to the tomb around this time, as do beads found at Bryn yr Hen Bobl and Dyffryn Ardudwy, although these latter examples might date to the Roman period. Perhaps these were chance losses from necklaces or bracelets, or perhaps they were simple offerings from visitors who wanted to leave a little of themselves behind.

STONEHENGE

Stonehenge in Wiltshire, drawn by William Stukeley in 1722. The bluestones from the Preseli Hills are the smaller stones set in front of the massive trilithons © The National Museum of Wales

Several hundred years after the end of megalithic tomb construction, around 2600 BC, at least eighty stones each weighing up to four tonnes were taken from the Preseli Hills and transported over 200 kilometres to Stonehenge in Wiltshire, where they eventually formed the inner circle and horseshoe at the site. The route probably involved transportation on rafts around the coast of south Wales, along the Bristol Avon and the Rivers Wylye and Avon. However, for many kilometres there would have been no option but to drag the stones across the land with brute force. It was a feat that would no doubt have astonished the builders of the megalithic tombs.

Pottery and coins from the Roman period have been found at several tombs, for example at Penywyrlod (Llanigon), where a coin of the emperor Crispus (AD 317-326) and glass beads that probably dated from the time of the Roman occupation were found. In the case of fragments of jars from the late second or early third century AD found at Tinkinswood, the excavator John Ward suggested that they could once have held cremations - continuing the tradition of burial at the site. However, the Romanist Evan Chapman thinks it more likely that they are simply household waste dropped on the cairn for convenience, although the discovery of a Roman gaming die at the same site hints at less practical activities. Not all tombs passed through the Roman

occupation so easily. At Din Dryfol, it is likely that the destruction of the site was begun in earnest during this time, with the discovery of iron slag suggesting that the tomb was used as a place for ironworking.

Several tombs in Wales have names linking them to early medieval saints. Carreg Samson and Ffyst Samson in Pembrokeshire were named after the sixth-century Saint Samson; the latter tomb is now known more widely as Trellysycoed. Ty Illtyd is named after the sixth- or seventh-century saint. These names were probably given to the tombs long after the deaths of the saints, though at Ty Illtyd there is evidence that hints at a role for the tomb during the early medieval period (the fifth to eleventh centuries AD). There is a view that this tomb was used as a hermitage and gathered its name as a result. The presence of carved crosses (among other motifs) on several of the chamber stones has been cited in support of this claim. The archaeologist and folklorist Leslie Grinsell regarded this as unlikely given the small size of the tomb, but he did consider that the carvings might have been the work of Christian pilgrims or, since the tomb is on a parish boundary, that they might have been added during parish perambulations - the walking of the parish boundaries to ensure they were remembered and maintained. In either case, he was willing to consider that Ty Illtyd was evidence of early Christian interest in megalithic tombs.

The British hero King Arthur has also been linked in folk-memory to several tombs, such as Carreg Coetan Arthur, Arthur's Stone and two Coetan Arthurs in Pembrokeshire, but there is no credible link between the Arthur of post-Roman Britain and the tombs. His name is likely to have been invoked simply as an explanation of the apparently super-human effort involved in raising the capstone. At Arthur's Stone, the King has to vie with another Welsh hero, St David, for a role in the tomb's folklore. Here the capstone is credited to Arthur's tossing it out as a stone from his shoe, while St David is held responsible for splitting the capstone in an effort to prove that it was not divine.

tombs and the early scholars
(seventeenth to nineteenth centuries)

The first written description of a tomb in Wales dates to 1603, when George Owen recorded his observations of Pentre Ifan, a site he marvelled 'farre passeth for biggnes and height [Arthur's Stone, Herefordshire] or [Llech yr Ast, Ceredigion] or anye other that I sawe, saveinge some in Stonedge upon Salisburie plaine'. He was writing some 5,000 years after the tomb was built and at a point in time when the purpose of such 'cromlechs', as they became known, was entirely forgotten. Owen's detailed description of the tomb represents the beginnings of the long process through which their origins and function have been rediscovered.

Throughout the seventeenth and eighteenth centuries, a growing number of travellers and antiquarians pondered the purpose of these cromlechs, largely in the context of biblical or classical sources, and formed a link between cromlechs and druids. This link was to remain throughout much of the nineteenth century, with serious thinkers proposing that capstones were druidic altars intended for human sacrifice, or that chambers were the houses of the druids. These scholars had in mind the kind of wild and powerful druids described by the historian Tacitus during the

Pentre Ifan in Pembrokeshire, published in 1865. George Owen, in 1603, wrote of the tomb: 'the stones whereon this is layed, are soe highe, that a man, on horsbacke, may well ride under it, without stowpinge'.

Courtesy of the Cambrian Archaeological Association

Roman conquest of Britain. In attributing cromlechs to this time, they were unwittingly trimming four thousand years off the lifespan of the tombs as well as misattributing their function.

On reaching Trevigneth, we examined some relics of Druidism, called Cromlechs ... our imaginations were led back to the period when the horrid rites of Druids, of whom at a very early period this island was a stronghold, were celebrated on this spot. Here the Druid priests once offered their dreadful sacrifices, and performed their idolatrous worship...

From Reminiscences of five days' rambles in the Isle of Holyhead in the month of September 1856, *by Thomas Jackson. An example of the popular nineteenth-century view of megalithic tombs as haunts of the Druids.*

Bron y Foel Isaf in Gwynedd forms an incongruous element in a network of recent dry stone walls.
© The National Museum of Wales (Kevin Thomas)

Although the early writers did not solve the riddle of the tombs, they did perform one very valuable service to later generations. Their records provide a description of many sites prior to their subsequent destruction. Furthermore, the publicity their activities generated in relation to these sites raised awareness that tombs were under threat from the on-going process of working the land.

Early descriptions of raised stones perched on uprights make it clear that many sites had already lost their covering cairns, and it is likely that many of the field walls in the vicinity of tombs are derived from this source. In other cases, antiquarian accounts record actual destruction. For example, Richard Fenton, writing in 1810, recorded that in around 1798 a tenant farmer had blasted away two legs from one of the chambers at St Elvies in Pembrokeshire and carried them away. Similarly, Edward Laws writing in 1888 noted that a tomb at Ffynnon Druidion in the same county was removed because a tenant 'grudged the land on which it stood'. Some damage recorded by the antiquarians was unwitting, albeit fuelled by a disregard for the tomb itself. For example, in the early nineteenth century a tenant lit a bonfire on top of the chamber at Ty Newydd to welcome his landlord home, resulting in a crack through the surviving capstone. While the stories recorded by these early writers are saddening, they do at least have forensic value.

N.W. View of the Cromlech at Plas Newydd Anglesey

H Longueville Jones. del

J. H. Le Keux Sc.

W. View of the Cromlech at Presaddfedd near Bodedern Anglesey

excavating the tombs
(nineteenth century to the present day)

As the number of people interested in the cromlech question grew, the range of methods used to study them also developed. Initially, it seems that most visitors were content to record the sites as they saw them. Later scholars attempted to add to these descriptions with excavation.

The well-known Wiltshire antiquarian Richard Colt Hoare was one of the first to start this process of excavation. On 26 May 1804 he and a few friends shifted one of the capstones at Gwernvale and proceeded to dig beneath it to see what the chamber contained. Their work was inconclusive. From this time on, the digging of tomb chambers became a common practice. Many such events have gone unrecorded, only to be rediscovered through later controlled excavation of a badly damaged chamber. However, the desultory accounts of a day spent digging are almost routine in the literature. For example, in 1853 a group of antiquarians dug at Capel Garmon, exposing the chambers but failing to add appreciably to understanding of the site. In about 1858, W. W. E. Wynne dug into Bryn yr Hen Bobl during a short visit, with the same conclusion. In 1865, the antiquarian Captain F. D. Lukis gained permission to dig at Bryn Celli Ddu, which he attacked in a three-day campaign. A week later, in writing to his father, another antiquarian, he observed '[t]he examination I made by digging was done too hurriedly'. Today, the same excavation would have taken months.

It is an unfortunate fact that so many well-intentioned people should have dug into tombs before the development of archaeological excavation techniques. The result is that evidence that would today be seen as of great value - broken pottery and bones, evidence for the sequence in which tombs were built - was all discarded or subsequently lost due to a lack of suitable museums. However, the work of early excavators across Britain and Ireland did begin to reveal patterns in the remains dug from tombs. Little was found to support the theory of druid homes or altars, while the frequency with which human bone was discovered revealed that these were tombs. In Wales, this view was not met with universal support, and indeed it was hotly debated

Tombs at Plas Newydd and Presaddfed in Anglesey, in the mid-nineteenth century. At this time, megalithic monuments were becoming increasingly popular as picturesque objects - a factor that no doubt saved many from destruction.

Courtesy of the Cambrian Archaeological Association

in the pages of the Welsh archaeological journal *Archaeologia Cambrensis* is almost from its first issue in 1846. To the authors of the day, there seems to have been something degrading in the view that these noble monuments were simply burial places. The passion with which this opinion was promoted can be seen through a quote from the *Cardiff and Merthyr Guardian* of 1 September 1849, following a visit to Tinkinswood by Irish scholar and proponent of tomb theory, Dr Todd:

> *The ancient badge of our nation, upon which our bards tell us the whole of our mythology hangs, must, after the facts adduced by Dr. Todd and others, undergo a most revolting wrench: we allude to the CROMLECH, the very pediment of bardism. While we write, we tremble! Hitherto all our bards have maintained, with one exception, that the Cromlech is an altar; and many and various are the theories founded on such a hypothesis. But shades of Dr. Owen Pugh. Iolo Morganwg and Carnhuanawc, what say you? Dr. Todd says they are tombs, charnel-houses, ovens to bake human bones in!*

Those who supported the view that these were druid monuments rallied to the cause and a fourteen-month exchange of letters followed in the newspaper. But without convincing evidence to support their case, there were less and less proponents of the druid theory during the latter part of the nineteenth century. The closing of the debate among scholars was effectively marked by the publication in 1915 of John Ward's work at Tinkinswood, in which he conclusively demonstrated through excavation that the site had been used as a tomb. Among the wider public, the link between druids and tombs has remained more persistent.

John Ward's work also marked a change in the approach to excavation at megalithic tombs. His thorough excavation and recording raised the standard for his contemporaries and made it increasingly unacceptable to treat the digging of a tomb as a social, rather than a scientific, event. Furthermore, his prompt and complete publication of his work also served to reinforce the developing view that without the writing up of discoveries, excavation was simply destruction.

Left: *John Ward, (centre), the excavator of the tomb at Tinkinswood, after the completion of his work in 1914. The diagonally placed stones to the right of the entrance are part of his reconstruction work. Through this sympathetic approach to renovation he has allowed modern visitors to clearly distinguish original from reconstruction, without greatly damaging the tomb's aesthetic, although he was less succesful with other aspects of the restoration work.*
© The National Museum of Wales

Right: *Gwernvale in Powys is set beside the A40, which, over the centuries, has meandered across the tomb's cairn. O. G. S. Crawford visited it in the early 1920s and recorded that at this time the chamber was 'used as a receptacle for old pails, bottles and jam jars, and is probably, from its position, in considerable danger of destruction'. The tomb was completely excavated between 1977 and 1978.*
© The National Museum of Wales (Kevin Thomas)

During the 1920s, W. J. Hemp conducted excellent excavations at Capel Garmon, Bryn Celli Ddu and Bryn yr Hen Bobl while he was working as Inspector of Ancient Monuments for Wales. Less distinguished was the contemporary work of C. E. Vulliamy at Penywyrlod (Llanigon) and the two tombs at Ffostyll. From the 1930s, W. F. Grimes began a series of first rate excavations at Ty-Isaf and then at Pentre Ifan. Grimes also undertook the first modern syntheses of megalithic tombs in Wales, resulting in publications that remain of great value to archaeologists today. The work of these pioneers no doubt inspired other scholars, including T. G. E. Powell, a future Professor at Liverpool University, Glyn Daniel, who later became Disney Professor at Cambridge University and Hubert Savory of the National Museum of Wales. The high standards they adopted have been maintained to the present through the excavation and publication of such sites as Benllech, Carreg Samson and Din Dryfol by Frances Lynch, Trefignath by C. Smith and Gwernvale by Bill Britnell. The work of these archaeologists has provided the foundation upon which this book, and many others, has been based.

preserving the tombs
(late nineteenth century to the present day)

Although the uncovering of the history of the tombs has been the driving force for most archaeologists from John Ward onwards, another factor also influenced the agenda of both the public and professionals from the start of the twentieth century.

Over the 6,000 years since they were built, megalithic tombs have been exposed to wind, rain, frost and, of course, gravity. Protected and insulated by their covering cairns, they seem to have been remarkably resilient to the elements. However, the removal of their cairns, whether to provide building materials or hardcore, served to reduce the structural stability of many of their chambers. This problem was no doubt exacerbated by amateur excavations, which undermined uprights and loosened the surrounding ground. The resulting danger of collapse might not have been immediately obvious, but over the years the weather, the intrusive roots of shrubs and trees and the underground tunnels of rats, mice and rabbits all served to destabilize the chambers. By the latter part of the nineteenth century, these problems were being recognized at many sites. The result was a growing call for the protection of tombs against further damage.

In 1882, the first piece of legislation designed to protect ancient monuments from wanton destruction by landowners, vandals or well-intentioned but ill-prepared archaeologists was passed by Parliament. The Ancient Monuments Act was intended to protect monuments of all types, and threatened up to a £5 fine (about £325 today) plus repair costs or up to one month's hard labour to those who damaged any monument listed on an approved schedule. In Wales, the only monuments to be proposed in the first schedule were the megalithic tombs of Plas Newydd in Anglesey, Arthur's Stone on Gower and Pentre Ifan in Pembrokeshire.

In the years that followed, all of the megalithic tombs in Wales were afforded legal protection under this and subsequent Acts of Parliament. Today, the penalty for disturbing a Scheduled Ancient Monument without consent is a fine or six months in

Above left: *Sweyne's Howe North on Gower. Without the protection of its covering mound, this chamber has collapsed in on itself, the rear stone falling forward and the capstone sliding back.*
© The National Museum of Wales (Kevin Thomas)

Above right: *Pentre Ifan in Pembrokeshire. In 1936, the capstone was in danger of collapse, making the addition of these temporary supports an urgent necessity until the stones could be made safe in the 1950s.*
Cadw, crown copyright

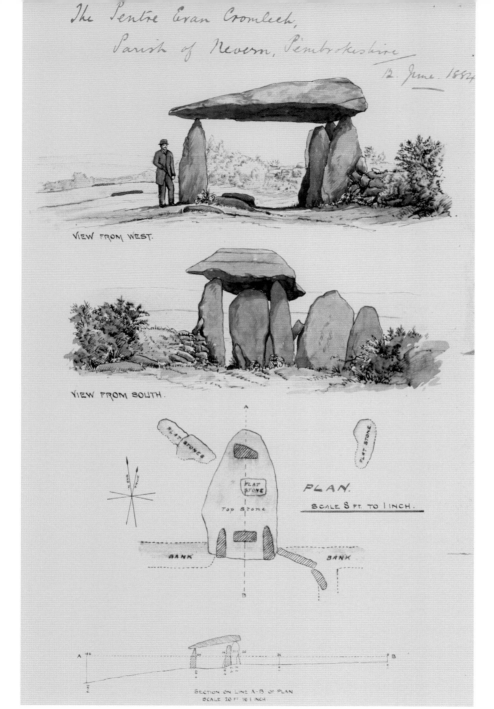

The Pentre Evan Cromlech,
Parish of Nevern, Pembrokeshire
12. June. 1884

VIEW FROM WEST.

VIEW FROM SOUTH.

FLAT STONES

FLAT STONE

PLAN.

FLAT STONE

Top Stone

SCALE 8 FT. TO 1 INCH.

BANK

BANK

SECTION ON LINE A-B OF PLAN
SCALE 20 FT TO 1 INCH.

On 8 June 1884 Pentre Ifan was visited by Lieutenant-General Pitt Rivers, one of the founders of modern archaeology, and Britain's first Inspector of Ancient Monuments. This sketch illustrates the condition of the site at the time of his visit. Twelve days later, the tomb was placed in the care of the State under the terms of the Ancient Monuments Act.

prison - or both. In Wales, scheduled monument consents are issued by Cadw.

Although protection has been effective in limiting the amount of deliberate damage caused to megalithic tombs, preventing systematic decay needs more active measures. For example, when John Ward dug at Tinkinswood he did so because the chamber capstone had noticeably slipped. At the conclusion of his excavation he had a brick pillar built to prop the capstone up and prevent further damage, but he was not present when the work was undertaken and he later recorded his disappointment at the large size of the resultant pillar. A similarly disfiguring brick pillar was inserted for the same reason beneath the capstone at Ty Newydd by C. W. Phillips in 1935. Although these pillars detract from the ambience of the tombs, they have both prevented collapse so far.

The stabilising of dangerous chambers has been a prime motivation in the excavation of many of Wales's tombs. Pentre Ifan was conserved during a programme of work undertaken between 1936-7 and 1958-9, after the chamber had become unsafe. Most of W. J. Hemp's excavations were undertaken for the same reason. The benefit of conducting thorough excavations prior to conservation work has been to allow the possibility of reconstructing tombs where the original features have been lost to view. In most cases, these reconstructions have been undertaken with considerable sympathy and with care to ensure that people are not misled as to what is original and what is not. For example, at Capel Garmon, Hemp restored the upper layers of drystone walling at the tombs to match the original walls beneath. In so doing, he was careful to drill holes in the lowermost line of replacement stones to ensure that a distinction could be made in future. Ward employed a similar technique at Tinkinswood, where restored walling is laid in a herring bone fashion to contrast with the original flat courses. At Pentre Ifan, Grimes marked out the line of missing stones down the length of the cairn using low concrete markers, clearing back the cairn sides to help the visitor visualize the site. More substantial reconstructions have taken place at Bryn Celli Ddu and Barclodiad Y Gawres. At the first tomb, the low cairn has been rebuilt over the passage and chamber to increase the ambience for the visitor. At the second, the chambers have been enclosed within a concrete dome,

*The Archaeology
Store at the National
Museum Cardiff.*

© The National Museum
of Wales (Kevin Thomas)

which serves the double purpose of recreating the experience of entering a darkened space and protecting the fragile carvings from exposure to the elements.

In the majority of cases, the finds from Wales's megalithic tombs have been donated to the National Museum of Wales, where they form an internationally important research collection, and many of the highlights are on display in the galleries. Like the excavation of the tombs themselves, the care of these collections is an active process of stewardship. As scientific techniques and our understanding of the past have developed, it has proved possible to reanalyse many of these artefacts, providing fresh insight into the date of the monuments and the people who built them. As for the bodies of the tomb builders themselves, the tombs in which they were once buried are no longer safe from disturbance, and to bury them at another location using an unfamiliar ritual would involve a desecration no less significant than the one that led to their exhumation, so these, too, are preserved in the collections.

conclusion

This book has been written in the belief that megalithic tombs have an important place in the history of Wales. They are the nation's oldest standing structures, and deserve to be the starting point for any thorough architectural history of the country. Being the work of Wales's first farmers, they also have an important role in helping us to understand how our ancestors moved from a life of hunting and gathering towards the modern world of towns, agriculture and consumerism. Through their widely distributed forms - Cotswold-Severn, passage tomb and portal dolmen - they also demonstrate that the inhabitants of Wales had an international perspective long before the formation of Europe's nation states. Such insights make megalithic tombs a window on the past, and a mirror to our own times.

For many, however, the experience of visiting a megalithic tomb is a much more personal one. As was mentioned at the beginning of the book, tombs have a strong resonance for many people. Their antiquity is apparent, even though the exact date of their construction might be largely unknown beyond academic circles. They are undoubtedly marvellous, and richly deserving of the myths and folklore that surround them. They are places where the past can be felt. Compared to such an experience, details of history might not have much impact, indeed they might seem of secondary importance. But they offer a complementary view to be considered when seated beside a megalithic tomb on a summer's day. In its way, this historical view is no less mysterious and provocative than the monuments themselves. It does not offer precise answers to straightforward questions, there are no personalities to be discovered or clear motives to be unearthed. What archaeologists have discovered through these centuries of study is that the mystery of the tombs is never-ending. The more knowledge that is acquired, the more questions present themselves and the more entrancing the mystery and the hope for answers. In all this, the tombs themselves remain silent.

places to visit

Many of the tombs discussed in this book are accessible to visitors. A selection of the most visually impressive, by virtue of their setting or completeness, is given here. The location of each tomb is given by its Ordnance Survey National Grid Reference.

ANGLESEY

Barclodiad y Gawres
SH329707 (Pages 102 and 103)
The name translates as 'The Apronful of the Giantess', a wonderfully evocative name befitting this cliff-top passage tomb. Excavated in 1952 and 1953, the tomb chambers have been re-covered by a concrete dome. Although this detracts somewhat from the ambience of the site, the elaborate rock art on the passage walls provides ample compensation.

The tomb is kept locked, but a key is held locally to allow visitors access. For current access details, contact Cadw.

Bryn Celli Ddu
SH508702 (Pages 52 and 109)
This passage tomb has been restored to allow the visitor to experience the walk down the dark passageway into the dimly lit end chamber. Around the mound of the tomb can be seen the circular ditch, which raises questions for archaeologists - is it the remains of an earlier ceremonial monument, or an integral part of the tomb's design?

A replica of the pattern stone found during excavations in the 1920s can be seen on the site; the original is in the National Museum Cardiff.

Lligwy
SH501860 (Page 65)
This is an unusual tomb, formed by raising a massive slab of limestone to create a sunken chamber. This can still be entered, although the weight of stone above the visitor's head can make the experience distinctly oppressive.

Trefignath
SH259805 (Page 56)
The best preserved long cairn in Anglesey and one with a complex three-phase construction history. At the rear of the cairn, distinctive ledges cut into the bedrock are likely to be the remains of a quarry from which the tomb stone was derived.

NORTH-WEST

Dyffryn Ardudwy, Gwynedd
SH589228 (Page 90)
In the centre of this long cairn are the remains of an earlier portal dolmen, illustrating two building traditions in one visit.

NORTH-EAST

Capel Garmon, Conwy
SH817543 (Pages 54 and 73)
This tomb, built in the Cotswold-Severn style, was for a time used as a stable. Now sympathetically restored, it offers the visitor a good insight into a building tradition not otherwise known from this part of Wales, as well as the pleasure of a visit to a starkly beautiful location.

SOUTH-WEST

Arthur's Stone, Gower
SS491906 (Pages 66 and 70)
Although this tomb does not fall easily into traditional classifications of tomb form, it is worth a visit for its setting alone. Situated on Cefn Bryn, a ridge that runs down the centre of Gower, it overlooks the Llanrhidian Sands and offers views as far as the mountains of south Wales.

Carreg Samson, Pembrokeshire
SM848335 (Page 129)
This tomb is an example of the simple chambers that are common in south-west Wales. Its excavator, Frances Lynch, saw it as a simple passage tomb, an attribution that would link it with larger sites such as Bryn Celli Ddu.

Parc le Breos Cwm, Gower
SS537898 (Pages 74 and 96)
Set on the floor of a wooded valley, this small Cotswold-Severn tomb is overlooked by Cat Hole Cave, which was occupied by Ice Age hunters several thousand years before the tomb was built.

Pentre Ifan, Pembrokeshire
SN099370 (Pages 57 and 114)
This tomb remains the archetypal megalithic tomb in Wales. Built in the portal dolmen tradition, its massive slanting capstone is delicately balanced, creating the impression that it floats on air.

SOUTH-EAST

Gwernvale, Powys
SO211192 (Pages 91 and 135)
Although little remains of this Cotswold-Severn tomb except the chamber stones, the importance of this site for our understanding of the megalithic tombs of Wales makes it worth a visit. It is conveniently situated beside the A40.

Mynydd Troed, Powys
SO162284 (Page 65)
This badly damaged Cotswold-Severn tomb is set in the hills above Llangorse Lake. Worth a visit for the dramatic views, which were no doubt appreciated by the builders during its construction.

Tinkinswood, Vale of Glamorgan
ST092733 (Pages 54 and 135)
The capstone of this large and well-preserved Cotswold-Severn tomb is reputedly the largest in Britain. The chamber has been badly damaged on one side, but it is still possible to enter by the original entrance.

The impressive chamber at St Lythans is not far from Tinkinswood and is well worth visiting at the same time (ST100723).

National Museum Cardiff
Cathays Park, Cardiff CF10 3NP
Exhibitions include artefacts from several megalithic tombs. The study collection includes material from:
Anglesey Barclodiad y Gawres, Bryn Celli Ddu, Bryn yr Hen Bobl, Din Dryfol, Lligwy, Pant y Saer, Trefignath, Ty Newydd.
Carmarthenshire Morfa Bychan, Twlc y Filiast.
Conwy Capel Garmon.
Denbighshire Tyddyn Bleiddyn.
Gower Parc le Breos Cwm.
Gwynedd Dyffryn Ardudwy.
Pembrokeshire Carreg Samson, Pentre Ifan.
Powys Ffostyll North and South, Gwernvale, Mynydd Troed, Penywyrlod, Penywyrlod (Llanigon), Pipton, Ty Illtyd, Ty-Isaf.
Vale of Glamorgan St Lythans, Tinkinswood.

further reading

Catalogue of the Mesolithic and Neolithic collections in the National Museums & Galleries of Wales, by Steve Burrow. National Museum Wales Books (2003).
Includes lists of the artefacts discovered in Wales's megalithic tombs and discussion of their importance.

Long Barrows of the Cotswolds and surrounding areas, by Timothy Darvill. Tempus Publishing (2004).
An important review of Cotswold-Severn tombs.

Megalithic tombs and long barrows in Britain, by Frances Lynch. Shire Publications (1997).
A useful overview of the various types of tombs in Britain, as well as an introduction to the terminology archaeologists use in studying them.

Places of special virtue: megaliths in the Neolithic landscapes of Wales, by Vicki Cummings and Alasdair Whittle. Oxbow Books (2004).
A study of all the megalithic tombs in Wales, with particular reference to their position in the landscape and the views that can be enjoyed from them.

Prehistoric Anglesey: the archaeology of the island to the Roman conquest, by Frances Lynch.
Anglesey Antiquarian Society (1991).
Summarizes the evidence from the island's tombs in a highly readable narrative.

Prehistoric funerary and ritual monuments. Cadw (2005).
An introduction to the work that is undertaken to preserve this important fragment of Wales's prehistoric heritage.

The chambered tombs of south-west Wales, by Christopher Thompson Baker. Oxbow Books (1992).
A useful gazetteer of the tombs of Carmarthenshire and Pembrokeshire.

glossary

Adze
A woodworking tool similar to an axe, but with the blade turned at right angles so it can be used to shave timbers.

Barrow
A mound of earth, turf, peat or sand covering a burial.

Cairn
A pile of stones forming a mound. Cairns have been used to cover tomb chambers, cists and graves, but some are simply a consequence of the removal of unwanted stones from fields.

Capstone
A stone slab that serves as the roof of a tomb chamber or cist.

Causewayed enclosure
A roughly circular enclosure consisting of one or more ditches broken in several places by causeways that allow access to the interior. They date to the time of the tomb builders and were built in England, Wales and parts of Ireland.

Cist
A stone-lined burial pit covered by a capstone.

Clyde tomb
A type of trapezoidal or rectangular cairn found in south-west Scotland. The chambers of these tombs consist of linked cells accessed from a forecourt at the wider end of the cairn. See page 55 for a map showing their distribution and an example of their typical shape.

Cotswold-Severn tomb
A type of tomb found in south-east Wales, Gloucestershire and surrounding counties. They typically have a trapezoidal cairn with access to the internal chambers via passages from the sides or the wider end of the cairn. See page 53 for a map showing their distribution and typical shape.

Court tomb
A type of trapezoidal or rectangular tomb found in Ireland and similar in form to the Clyde tombs of Scotland. Their distribution can be seen on page 55, along with an example of their shape.

Cremation
The practice of disposing of the dead by burning. The process reduces an average weight adult to between two and three kilograms of bone and dust.

Cromlech
A Welsh word for megalithic tombs. The word is first recorded in the name 'Maen y gromlegh' (now known as Pentre Ifan), which appears in George Owen's Description of Pembrokeshire (1603), but is known to have been applied more generally to monuments of this type from the eighteenth century.

Dolmen
A French word for megalithic tombs (dolmen = 'table stone'), which has been used in Wales since the nineteenth century, although it is uncommon today.

Earthen long barrow
A type of tomb common in areas where stone is in short supply, such as southern and eastern England. Earthen long barrows typically have trapezoidal mounds with a number of burials placed beneath the larger end.

Excarnation
The defleshing of the body before burial.

Facade
Walling, whether drystone, megalithic or timber, at the front of a tomb.

Harris line
Mineralized lines at the end of long bones that indicate periods when the individual's growth was arrested.

Inhumation
The burial of a complete corpse (see also excarnation).

Kerb
The stone footing or walling surrounding a cairn or mound.

Lintel
A wooden beam or stone slab forming the top of a door or archway. The term is normally applied to the slabs resting on the uprights at Stonehenge.

Megalith
Any large stone used in construction. The term is typically applied to the stones used in the construction of tomb chambers,

standing stones and larger stone circles.

Midden
A mound chiefly made of organic rubbish.

Neolithic
The archaeological term for the period of time from the first appearance of farming to the introduction of metals. In Britain, the Neolithic spans 4000-2500 BC and includes the age of the tomb builders.

Palisade
A line of upright timbers forming a wall or fence.

Passage tomb
A type of tomb consisting of a round mound containing a passageway leading to a central chamber. See page 51 for a map showing their distribution and examples of their form.

Portal dolmen
A type of burial chamber with an H-shaped entranceway, often with a boldly sloping capstone. Pentre Ifan is a classic example. See page 58 for a map showing their distribution.

Pyre
A pile of wood upon which a corpse is burnt.

Radiocarbon dating
Carbon occurs in all plants and animals, with a tiny fraction being the radioactive form, carbon 14. This unstable carbon decays at a steady rate - halving in quantity every 5,568 years. While the organism is alive, the quantity of carbon 14 is replenished from food and water; after death it decreases. Radiocarbon dating measures the concentration of carbon 14 surviving in a sample: the smaller the concentration, the older the sample.

The date obtained is then calibrated against graphs produced from the radiocarbon dates of organisms of known age, for example ancient oak trees found in peat bogs, to produce a date in calendar years, BC or AD.

Shell-midden
A rubbish heap created from sea shells that have been discarded after the edible part has been removed.

Standing stone
A large freestanding upright stone. It seems the tomb builders erected some standing stones, but the majority of the more than 300 found in Wales are more recent.

Stone circle
A circle of upright stones. The stone circle at Bryn Celli Ddu is the work of the tomb builders, but the vast majority in Wales are more recent.

Wrasse
A family of brightly coloured fish. The Ballan wrasse is found in the eastern Atlantic Ocean and can grow to more than 60 centimetres.

index